Michael James Cox & Tom O'Connell in
association with Park Theatre present

RAISING
MARTHA

A Comedy

by David Spicer

║SAMUEL FRENCH║

samuelfrench.co.uk

THINKING ABOUT PERFORMING A SHOW?

There are thousands of plays and musicals available to perform from Samuel French right now, and applying for a license is easier and more affordable than you might think

From classic plays to brand new musicals, from monologues to epic dramas, there are shows for everyone.

Plays and musicals are protected by copyright law so if you want to perform them, the first thing you'll need is a license. This simple process helps support the playwright by ensuring they get paid for their work, and means that you'll have the documents you need to stage the show in public.

Not all our shows are available to perform all the time, so it's important to check and apply for a license before you start rehearsals or commit to doing the show.

LEARN MORE & FIND THOUSANDS OF SHOWS

Browse our full range of plays and musicals and find out more about how to license a show
www.samuelfrench.co.uk/perform

Talk to the friendly experts in our Licensing team for advice on choosing a show, and help with licensing
plays@samuelfrench.co.uk   020 7387 9373

Acting Editions

BORN TO PERFORM

Playscripts designed from the ground up to work the way you do in rehearsal, performance and study

---

Larger, clearer text for easier reading

Wider margins for notes

Performance features like character and props lists, sound and lighting cues, and more

---

+ CHOOSE A SIZE AND STYLE TO SUIT YOU

  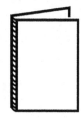

STANDARD EDITION

Our regular paperback book at our regular size

SPIRAL-BOUND EDITION

The same size as the Standard Edition, but with a sturdy, easy-to-fold, easy-to-hold spiral-bound spine

LARGE EDITION

A4 size and spiral bound, with larger text and a blank page for notes opposite every page of text. Perfect for technical and directing use

LEARN MORE | samuelfrench.co.uk/actingeditions

MUSIC USE NOTE

Licensees are solely responsible for obtaining formal written permission from copyright owners to use copyrighted music in the performance of this play and are strongly cautioned to do so. If no such permission is obtained by the licensee, then the licensee must use only original music that the licensee owns and controls. Licensees are solely responsible and liable for all music clearances and shall indemnify the copyright owners of the play(s) and their licensing agent, Samuel French, against any costs, expenses, losses and liabilities arising from the use of music by licensees. Please contact the appropriate music licensing authority in your territory for the rights to any incidental music.

IMPORTANT BILLING AND CREDIT REQUIREMENTS

If you have obtained performance rights to this title, please refer to your licensing agreement for important billing and credit requirements.

Raising Martha was first performed at Park Theatre, London on 12th January 2017 with the following cast:

Marc..TOM BENNETT

Roger Duffy...JULIAN BLEACH

Gerry Duffy...STEPHEN BOXER

Jago...JOEL FRY

Caro Duffy..GWYNETH KEYWORTH

Clout...JEFF RAWLE

Director...MICHAEL FENTIMAN

Set and Costume Designer................................REBECCA BROWER

Lighting Designer...ELLIOT GRIGGS

Sound Designer..MAX PAPPENHEIM

Casting Director...ANNE VOSSER

Costume Supervisor...RYAN WALKLETT

Assistant Director...ROSA CROMPTON

Production Manager.......................................SIMON STREETING

Fight Director..BRET YOUNT

Props Maker...JAYNE O'HANLON

Mask Maker...ISA SHAW-ABULAFIA

Producer...MICHAEL JAMES COX

Producer...TOM O'CONNELL

General Manager.................TOM O'CONNELL PRODUCTIONS

Company Stage Manager On Book............ **ALICE JENKINS**

Assistant Stage Managers............ **EMILY HUMPHRYS**
ZARA JANMOHAMED
GERALDINE DONALDSON

Marketing............ **WILL MAIDWELL**
FOR MAIDWELL MARKETING
PR............ **ARABELLA NEVILLE-ROLFE FOR TARGET LIVE**
Branding Design............ **TANGERINE**
Filming and Editing............ **WILL AUSTIN**
Video Animation............ **BRUNO COLLINS**
Production Photography............ **DARREN BELL**
Set Construction............ **SET BLUE SCENERY**
Lighting Supplied by............ **PRG**
Sound Supplied by............ **STAGE SOUND SERVICES**
Blood Supplier............ **RC-ANNIE LIMITED**
Insurance............ **LIN POTTER FOR WRIGHTSURE**

For Tom O'Connell Productions
Executive Producer............ **TOM O'CONNELL**
General Manager............ **DEBBIE HICKS**
Production Coordinator............ **MATTHEW FORBES**
Production Associate............ **JACOB JACKSON**
Production Assistant............ **ZOE WELDON**
(STAGE ONE APPRENTICE)
Head of Accounts............ **MARK REYNOLDS**
Legal............ **NEIL ADLEMAN FOR HARBOTTLE & LEWIS LLP**
Shareholders............ **RAY COONEY OBE & STEPHEN HALL**

CAST

Tom Bennett – Marc

Theatre credits include: *Swallows & Amazons* (Bristol Old Vic); *An Incident At The Border* (Finborough Theatre); *Pushing Up Poppies* (Theatre 503).

Film credits include: *Life On The Road* (Ricky Gervais); *Mascots* (Christopher Guest); *Love & Friendship* (Whit Stillman).

Television credits include: *Rebellion 2* (RTE); *Drunk History 3*; *Crackanory; Murder Prevention* (Tiger Aspect); *Tina & Bobby; Life Begins* (ITV); *Fungus and the Bogey Man* (Imaginarium Studios); *Top Coppers* (BBC Three); *Save The Date* (ABC/CBS); *Family Tree* (HBO); *Upstairs Downstairs; Silent Witness; My Hero* (BBC); *Phoneshop; Minder; Pulling; Silver River; The Bill* (Talkback Thames); *EastEnders* (BBC); *Ultimate Force; Midsomer Murders* (Bentley Productions); *Foyle's War* (Greenlit Productions).

Julian Bleach – Roger Duffy

Theatre credits include: *The Grinning Man* (Bristol Old Vic); *Every Good Boy Deserves Favour* (National Theatre); *Oliver!* (Cameron Macintosh Ltd.); *Anthony and Cleopatra* (RSC); *The Importance of Being Earnest* (Oxford Stage Company); *The Firework Maker's Daughter* (Sheffield Crucible); *Cabaret* (Chichester Festival Theatre); *A Midsummer Night's Dream* (English Shakespeare Company); *The Government Inspector* (West Yorkshire Playhouse); *Gormenghast* (David Glass New Mime Ensemble); *Dracula* (London Bubble Theatre); *Macbeth* (Cheltenham Everyman Theatre).

Television credits include: *Close To The Enemy; Doctor Who; This Is Jinsy II; The Borgais I, II & III; Ripper Street; MI High; Psychoville; The Sarah Jane Adventures; Torchwood; Frankenstein; John Adams; Come Fly With Me; Riot at the Rite.*

Film credits include: *Avengers: Age Of Ultron; Emperor; DXM; Remainder; Les Miserables; Anonymous; Lecture 21; Badinage; The Fall; The Brothers Grimm; Topsy-Turvy; Beg; The Fool.*

Radio credits include: *Gospel; Faustus; Regime Change* (BBC Radio).

Stephen Boxer – Gerry Duffy

Theatre credits include: *Titus in Titus Andronicus, William Tyndale in Written on the Heart, Archbishop Aguiar in The Heresy of Love, Petruchio in The Taming Of The Shrew, Thomas Hobbs in The Tragedy of Thomas Hobbs, Bartholomew Fair, Measure for Measure, Twelfth Night, The Herbal Bed, The White Devil, The General From America, The Duchess Of Malfi, Barbarians, Richard III, Rousseau's Tale* (RSC); *King Lear, The Holy Rosenbergs, Aristocrats, Power, Volpone, At Our Table, Once In A While The Odd Thing Happens* (National Theatre); *The Hypochondriac, A Chaste Maid In Cheapside* (Almeida).

Other London theatre: William Adams in *Anjin: The Shogun and The English Samurai* (Sadler's Wells): William Tyndale in *Written on the Heart* (The Duchess): *Hayfever* (The Rose Kingston): *The Clearing* (The Bush, won London Fringe Award for Best Actor); *Antartica* (Savoy Theatre); *Six Characters Looking for an Author* (Young Vic); *The Cocktail Party* (The Phoenix Theatre); *The Devil & The Good Lord, Faith, Hope & Charity* (Lyric Hammersmith); *Measure for Measure* (Cheek By Jowl & Lyric Hammersmith & World Tour); *The Brothers Karamazov* (Russian Tour & West End)
UK theatre: *Regeneration* (Northampton); *Brighton Beach Memoirs, Love and Marriage, God and Stephen Hawking* (Theatre Royal, Bath); *Six Degrees of Separation* (Crucible, Sheffield); *The Alchemist* (Cambridge Theatre Co.); *Richard III Part 2, Music To Murder By* (Paines Plough).

Abroad: *Julius Caesar* (Leicester Haymarket – India).

Television credits include: *Poldark; The Five; Agatha Raisin And The Potted Gardener; Lewis; Lucky Man; Humans; Life in Squares; Toast of London; The Honourable Woman; Foyle's War; Death in Paradise; Father Brown; Garrow's Law (3 series) Luther; Casualty; Breaking The Mould; Doctors; The Quatermass Experiment; Midsomer Murders; Cherished; Life Begins; Silent Witness; Daziell and Pascoe; Trail & Retribution;*

Rosemary & Thyme; Ultimate Force; Trust; Murphy's Law; Sons and Lovers; In Deep; Blue Dove; Happy Monsters; Casualty; Rough Treatment; Grafters; Killer Net; The Bill; Karaoke; The Politician's Wife; Under The Hammer; Casualty; Prime Suspect; The Best Man To Die; Brookside; The Waterfall; Mooncat & Co.

Film credits include: *The Gatehouse, Ginger and Rosa, The Iron Lady, We are the Freaks, Children of Men, AKA, Mary Reilly, Carrington.*

Stephen has worked on numerous radio plays and has written two programmes for radio on China and Hong Kong. He also composes music for radio, television and theatre.

Joel Fry – Jago

Theatre credits include: *Public Enemy; Doctor Faustus* (Young Vic); *Wuthering Heights* (Theatre Royal York); *As You Like It* (Stoke New Vic); *Romeo and Juliet* (The Lost Theatre Co.)

Film credits include: *Paddington 2; Svengali; Wild Dog; Tamara Drewe; Exposed; Distant Mirage; Waiting for Exit Music; 10,000 BC.*
Television credits include: *Ordinary Lies; Death in Paradise* (BBC1); *You, Me and the Apocalypse* (NBC/Sky1); *Game of Thrones* (HBO/Sky1); *W1A; Twenty Twelve* (BBC2); *Plebs* (ITV2); *Trolled* (Sky1); *The Wrong Door; White Van Man* (BBC3).

Gwyneth Keyworth – Caro Duffy

Theatre credits include: *As You Like It / The Heresy of Love* (The Globe Theatre); *The Life and Times of Fanny Hill* (Bristol Old Vic; *Café Cariad* (National Youth Theatre of Wales); *Sick Room* (National Youth Theatre); *Tits/Teeth* (National Youth Theatre).

Television credits include: *Wasted, Misfits, Poor Monkeys; Dr Thorne; The Suspicions of Mr Whicher; The Wizard's Sleeve; The Vodka Diaries; Case Histories; Joe Mistry; Midsomer Muder; The Great Outdoors; The Sarah Jane Adventures; Royal*

Wedding; Framed; Merry Widows.

Film credits include: *Elfie Hopkins: Cannibal Hunter; Closer to The Moon; Copier.*

Jeff Rawle – Clout

Theatre credits include: *A Room With a View* (Bath Theatre Royal); *Lawrence After Arabia* (Hampstead Theatre); *Waiting For Godot* (Sheffield Crucible); *High Society* (The Old Vic); *Handbagged* (West End/Tricycle Theatre); *Cocktail Sticks* (National Theatre; *Excellent Choice* (Eye Saw Theatre); *The Power of Yes; Fram; Noises Off* (National Theatre); *Pornography* (Traverse Theatre); *King of Hearts* (Out of Joint); *Way to Heaven; Bent* (Royal Court Theatre); *The Caretaker* (Thorndike Theatre); *Once a Catholic* (Wyndham's Theatre); *Equus* (Aldwych Theatre).
Film credits include: *The Crucifixion; The Redistributors; Trimming Pablo; Harry Potter & The Goblet of Fire; Black Ball; Awayday; Laughterhouse; Rating Notman; A Hitch in Time; Correction Please; The Case of Marcel Duchamp; Crystal Gazing; Doctor and the Devils; The Life Story of Baal.*

Television credits include: *Lost Sitcoms – Steptoe and Son; An Adventure in Space and Time; Heading Out; Holby City; The Charles Dickens Show; Doc Martin; Spooks; My Dad's the Prime Minister* (BBC); *The Durrells* (Sid Gentle Films Ltd); *You, Me and Them* (Hat Trick Productions); *The Outcast* (Blue Print Productions); *88 Keys* (Big Talk Productions); *New Tricks* (Wall to Wall) *A Beautiful Day* (Objective Productions); *Hollyoaks* (Lime Pictures); *The Plot* (Blue Tiger Productions Ltd); *My Family* (DLT Entertainment); *The Sarah Jane Adventures* (DW Productions); *MI High* (Kudos Productions); *Secret Diary of a Call Girl* (Tiger Aspect); *Touch of Frost* (Yorkshire Television); *Ultimate Force* (Bentley Productions); *Minder* (Euston Films).

CREATIVE

Michael Fentiman – Director

Training: Bretton Hall and Mountview Academy.

Theatre credits include: The Taming of the Shrew; Titus Andronicus; Ahasverus (Royal Shakespeare Company); Babe (Polka Theatre/UK Tour); The War Has Not Yet Started (Drum Theatre, Plymouth; Sweeney Todd (Theatre Royal Stratford East); Minotaur (Clwyd Theatr Cymru/Polka Theatre); The Lion, the Witch and the Wardrobe (Kensington Palace Gardens. Co-director with Rupert Goold); Crackers (Belgrade Coventry); Spoonface Steinberg (Clwyd Theatr Cymru/Glasgow Citizens/ Tour); Blue/Orange (Cockpit); Guy (Pleasance); East (Basingstoke/Tour); Ajax (Cyprus Tour); Romeo and Juliet (Playhouse Theatre); The Comedy of Errors; Robin Hood; Jack and the Beanstalk (Cambridge Arts Theatre); Clybourne Park; In Arabia We'd All Be Kings; As You Like It (RADA); Dracula (LAMDA); I Love You; You're Perfect; Now Change (RWCMD); Made in Dagenham (Adelphi Theatre. Associate Director to Rupert Goold).

Event credits include: A Feast with the Gods; By Royal Command (Almeida); Opening Ceremony of the RST (Royal Shakespeare Company).

Radio credits include: *Hatton Cross* (Urban Scrawl).

Television credits include: *Shakespeare Unlocked* (BBC/Cultural Olympiad).

Rebecca Brower – Set and Costume Designer

Rebecca studied at Central School of Speech and Drama.

Rebecca was the winner of The Stage Newspaper Design Award and The Equity Young Members Bursary Award in 2012. Rebecca was on the Design Team for the Opening and Closing Ceremonies for the London 2012 Olympic and Paralympic Games and has also designed corporate events and dinners at

The National Theatre. Rebecca was Associate Designer on the Great North Run Opening Ceremony in 2014. Rebecca most recently made the short list for The Old Vic 12 Designer.

Theatre Credits include: *The Boys In The Band; 4000 Days* (Park Theatre); *The House* (GDIF); *All or Nothing* (The Vaults, UK Tour); *The Devil Speaks True* (Waterloo Vaults); *Beauty and the Beast* (ArtsEd); *Coming Up* (Watford Palace Theatre); *Treasure* (Finborough Theatre); *Genius Bar* (Pleasance, UK Tour); *Beegu* (Arts Depot); *Dad Dancing* (BAC); *Struileag* (Glasgow Green); *Idylls of The King; Lord of the Flies* (Oxford (Oxford Playhouse); *Tender Loving Care* (The New Theatre Royal, Portsmouth); *Canterbury Tales; Heartbreak Beautiful* (Watford Palace Theatre); *Pursue Me* (The Place); *Jack and the Beanstalk* (Southwark Playhouse); *This Child* (The Bridewell Theatre); *Hamlet* (The Rose Theatre, Bankside. OffWest End Nomination, Best Set Design), *I DO I DO* (Riverside Studios).

Elliot Griggs – Lighting Designer

Training: RADA

Recent lighting design credits include: *Fleabag* (Soho Theatre/ UK Tour); *Kiki's Delivery Service* (Southwark Playhouse); *Sheppey, buckets* (Orange Tree); *Fool For Love* (Found 111); *Romeo and Juliet, Pigeon English* (NYT/Ambassadors Theatre); *Don't Wake the Damp, He Had Hairy Hands; The Boy Who Kicked Pigs* (Lowry, Salford/UK Tour); *Educating Rita* (Hull Truck); *The Night Watch* (Royal Exchange); *The Box of Photographs* (Polka Theatre); *The Sugar-Coated Bullets of the Bourgeoisie* (Arcola Theatre/HighTide Festival); *The Argument; Deluge* (Hampstead Theatre); *Martha, Josie and the Chinese Elvis* (Hull Truck/Bolton Octagon); *Yen* (Royal Court/Royal Exchange); *Forget Me Not* (Bush Theatre); *Pomona* (National Theatre/Royal Exchange/Orange Tree Theatre); *Lampedusa* (Soho Theatre/HighTide Festival/Unity Theatre, Liverpool); *Hansel and Gretel* (Belgrade Theatre Coventry); Benefit (Cardboard Citizens); *Henry IV* (Associate Lighting Designer; Donmar Warehouse); *CommonWealth* (Almeida Theatre); *Defect* (Perfect Pitch); *Marching On Together* (Old Red Lion); *John Ferguson, The Soft of her Palm, And I and*

Silence (Finborough Theatre); Infanticide (Camden People's Theatre); *Belleville Rendez-Vous* (Greenwich Theatre); *Meat* (Theatre503); *Lagan* (Oval House Theatre).

Event Design includes: *Height of Winter; The Single-Opticon; Alcoholic Architecture* (Bompas and Parr).

Awards: Best Lighting Designer (Off West End Awards 2014), New Talent in Entertainment Lighting (Association of Lighting Designers 2014), Francis Reid Award (Association of Lighting Designers 2011).

Max Pappenheim – Sound Designer

Theatre includes: *The Children* (Royal Court), *Labyrinth* (Hampstead Theatre), *Ophelias Zimmer* (Schaubühne, Berlin and Royal Court), *Sheppey, Blue/Heart, Little Light, The Distance* (Orange Tree Theatre, Richmond), *The Gaul* (Hull Truck), *Toast* (Park Theatre and 59E59 Theatres, New York), *Jane Wenham* (Out of Joint), *Waiting for Godot* (Sheffield Crucible), *My Eyes Went Dark* (Traverse, Edinburgh), *Cargo* (Arcola Theatre), *CommonWealth* (Almeida Theatre), *A Lovely Sunday for Creve Coeur* (Print Room), *Wink* (Theatre503), *Fabric, Invincible* (National Tours), *Spamalot, The Glass Menagerie, Strangers On A Train* (English Theatre, Frankfurt), *Kiki's Delivery Service, Johnny Got His Gun, Three Sisters, Fiji Land, Our Ajax* (Southwark Playhouse), *Mrs Lowry and Son* (Trafalgar Studios), *Martine, Black Jesus, Somersaults, The Fear of Breathing* (Finborough Theatre), *The Faction's Rep Season 2015* (New Diorama Theatre), *Shopera: Carmen* (Royal Opera House), *The Hotel Plays* (Langham Hotel).

As Associate, *The Island* (Young Vic), *Fleabag* (Soho Theatre).

Radio includes *Home Front* (BBC Radio 4).

Anne Vosser – Casting Director

Anne started casting in 1992 whilst at the Apollo Leisure Group. She has cast numerous West End and touring productions. She is currently casting with Take That for their 2017 Arena tour

Wonderland and an ITV Special.

Recent musical credits include: *The Life* directed by Michael Blakemore (Southwark Playhouse, London); *The Last Tango* (West End, Phoenix); *Guys and Dolls* (UK Tour), *Exposure* (St. James, London), *The Sessions – The Beatles at Abbey Road* (Royal Albert Hall); concert versions of *Follies* at the Royal Albert Hall starring Christine Baranski and *How To Succeed in Business Without Really Trying* at the Royal Festival Hall starring Jonathan Groff; Olivier nominated *Dance 'Til Dawn* (West End, Aldwych Theatre).

Recent play credits include: *Some Girl(s)*, *Raising Martha* (Park Theatre, London), *Stalking the Bogeyman* (Southwark Playhouse, London); The Old Vic New Voices Festival (The Old Vic); *The Mentalists* starring Stephen Merchant (West End, Wyndhams), *Barking In Essex* starring Lee Evans (West End, Wyndhams); *What The Butler Saw* (West End, Vaudeville); *Pygmalion* starring Alistair McGowan (UK Tour); and *Flare Path* (UK Tour).

www.vosser-casting.co.uk

Michael James-Cox – Producer

Michael James-Cox Productions was founded in 2014. Michael has had over 10 years of experience within the theatre industry and after having trained as an actor he has taken the step into producing.

His first show – *Impotent* was a sell-out success, followed by a co-production between Graeae Theatre Company and New Wolsey Theatre – *The Iron Man*. Since then Michael has honed his craft by working at Mark Goucher Productions Ltd. This has played an integral part in Michael's career, working on productions such as; *The Dresser, Million Dollar Quartet, Hairspray, Jeeves and Wooster, Slava's Snowshow, The King's Speech, The Vagina Monologues* and *A Chorus Line*.

Tom O'Connell – Producer

Current productions: *The Boys In The Band* (Vaudeville), *Million Dollar Quartet* (Royal Festival Hall & UK Tour); *Babe The Sheep-Pig* (Polka & UK Tour), Joe Orton's *Loot*, *Raising Martha* (Park Theatre), *The Miser* (Garrick); *Ray Cooney's Out Of Order* (UK Tour), *The Wedding Singer – Musical* (UK Tour).

Past productions: *The Boys In The Band* (Park Theatre & UK Tour), *Hairspray The Musical* (UK Tour), Alan Bennett's *Single Spies* (UK Tour), *Someone Who'll Watch Over Me* (Chichester Festival Theatre), *The King's Speech* (UK Tour 2015), *Ghost Stories* (Arts Theatre, West End 2014-2015), *Beautiful Thing 2015* (UK Tour), *Another Country* (Trafalgar Studios, West End/ UK Tour 2014); *Breeders* (St James Theatre, 2014); *Step 9 [Of 12]* (Trafalgar Studios, West End).

In development: A new stage adaptation of Annie Proulx's iconic *Brokeback Mountain*, a new stage adaptation of Zoe Heller's thriller *Notes On A Scandal* and a new revival of Ray Cooney's *Run For Your Wife*.

In 2013, Tom produced the critically acclaimed and award-winning production of Jonathan Harvey's *Beautiful Thing* starring Suranne Jones, marking the play's twentieth anniversary and is now available to download across the world as a HD filmed play; in partnership with DigitalTheatre.com

Tom trained as a producer at Fiery Angel LLP, funded by the fantastic Stage One new producers scheme, working on *The 39 Steps* (Criterion & UK Tour), *The Ladykillers* (Gielgud & UK Tour), *Ben Hur* with four actors (Newbury Playhouse / The Watermill), Olivier Award-winning *Goodnight Mister Tom* (Phoenix – West End & UK Tour), *Swallows & Amazons* (Vaudeville – West End & UK Tour), *Peppa Pig Live* (Criterion - West End & UK Tour), *Ben & Holly's Little Kingdom Live* (UK Tour).

www.tomocopro.com

The producers would like to extend special thanks to:

Michael Barfoot, Thom Brown, Guy Chapman, American Church, Ray Cooney, Sue Cox, Sean Foley, Mark Goucher, Stephen Hall, Emily Hickman, Graham Hubbard, Out Of Joint, Giles Rowland, Jonathan Russell, Jen Seymour and Mark Wild.

About Park Theatre

Park Theatre was founded by Artistic Director, Jez Bond. The building opened in May 2013 and, with two West End transfers, two National Theatre transfers and three national tours in its first two years, quickly garnered a reputation as a key player in the London theatrical scene. In 2015 Park Theatre received an Olivier nomination and won The Stage's Fringe Venue of the Year.

Park Theatre is a neighbourhood theatre with a global ambition.

We present world-class theatre, collaborating with the finest existing and emerging talent. We programme classics through to new writing, distinguished by strong narrative drive and powerful emotional content. We produce both in-house and in partnership with the most excellent existing and emerging producers, with whom we endeavour to provide an unparalleled level of support.

With a welcoming and nurturing environment we want Park Theatre to be accessible to everyone, within our diverse community and beyond – and through affordable ticket pricing and outreach programmes we aim to engage with those with little or no experience of theatre.

We aim to be a beacon for all and an ambassador for theatre worldwide.

"A five-star neighbourhood theatre." Independent

As a registered charity [number 1137223] with no public subsidy, we rely on the kind support of our donors and volunteers. To find out how you can get involved visit parktheatre.co.uk

ABOUT THE AUTHOR

David Spicer's stage plays include *Superheroes* (The King's Head, London and Edinburgh Festival) *Long Live the Mad Parade* (Ashcroft Theatre, Croydon) and *Stop!...the Play* (Trafalgar Studios, London).

Raising Martha is dedicated, with love,
To Lesley, Lewis and Daniel

CHARACTERS

In order of speaking:

MARC – An idealistic animal rights activist. 20–25. He is kind-hearted but easily manipulated.

JAGO – A hard-line animal rights activist. 25–30. He is angry and inflexible in his beliefs and for all his talk of a cruelty-free life, enjoys seeing people suffer.

CLOUT – A policeman. 50s. Not terribly bright. He enjoys the trappings of his authority but is complacent about its responsibilities.

GERRY – A frog farmer. 45–50. A reclusive thinker who's natural cynicism about life has always stopped him interacting with life.

ROGER – Gerry's brother. 40–45. A man who has struggled to make a good life for himself and his family but who has been disappointed and is bitter about it.

CARO – Roger's daughter. 25–30. A manipulative young woman who will use anyone and anything to get what she wants.

The action takes place in a country graveyard.
The kitchen of Gerry and Roger's frog farm and Jago and Marc's rented flat.

TIME

The present

ACT ONE

A graveyard in the middle of the night

A grave is open and flashlights are seen, shining up from inside. A pick axe and a spade appear at regular intervals, throwing dirt out.

Two voices are heard from below...

MARC Are we there yet?

JAGO No.

MARC So how much further? Do you think she's still in here?

JAGO She's been buried for five years. Of course she's still in here! The gravestone says 'Not Dead Just Resting' but they're kidding no one.

MARC I just thought we'd have got to her by now.

JAGO Just keep digging.

MARC I am digging. But...

JAGO Dig! We are on a clandestine operation here! Stealth and silence are vital.

MARC Okay.

JAGO Shut up!!! ...What was that?

MARC What was what?

JAGO That.

MARC What?

JAGO Noise.

MARC Noise?

JAGO Noise. I heard something.

MARC What noise?

JAGO A noise.

MARC If you're winding me up...

JAGO *(loudly)* There was a noise!

MARC Ssssh!

> **MARC**'s *head appears from the grave. He wears a toy frog mask. He looks around. After a few seconds* **JAGO**'s *head appears from the grave. He also wears a frog mask.*

JAGO Can you see anything?

MARC No. It's this bloody mask.

JAGO Take it off!

> *They both take off their masks.*

MARC Probably just a wild animal.

JAGO You mean a "liberated" animal. One of the fortunate few who can live their life with dignity, free from the tyranny of human oppression.

MARC Yes. One of them.

> *They heave themselves up out of the grave and look around.*

JAGO What's the matter with you?

MARC What do you think? We're digging up an old lady. Also I'm knackered. I'm a vegan. I'm not cut out for manual labour.

JAGO Following a cruelty-free diet shouldn't impede your fitness or stamina.

MARC I know, I know. I've read the pamphlets. Right now I wish I'd eaten them as well. Jago...

JAGO *Don't*...use my real name. Not when we're on an operation.

MARC Jago's your real name?

JAGO It's my cadre name. My nom de guerre. It identifies me to the authorities.

MARC So why can't I use it on an operation?

JAGO Because... It also happens to be the name on my library card. So zip it.

MARC Can I call you your real, *real* name? What is your real name?

JAGO I'm not telling. Why talk so much?

MARC I need to talk.

JAGO Let's dig.

JAGO jumps back into the grave and crashes through the coffin timbers.

Marc! I've found her. Hand me down the sack.

MARC *is transfixed with horror, staring down into the grave.*

Good morning Mrs Duffy. Sleep well did you? Marc, get down here quick.

MARC *faints and crashes into the grave.*

JAGO *yells at him.*

The lights change to daylight and Detective Inspector CLOUT *climbs out of the grave, clutching a human femur. He is tangled up in police tape.*

CLOUT Well. What can I say? Country coppers like myself are well versed in the dark bucolic underbelly of the church fete and the homely bonhomie which masks the seething cauldron of English village life. I can say that much. But this? Well, what can I say? No one likes being made a monkey of, particularly by people who appear to hold monkeys in higher regard than they do people. But who in their right mind could have foreseen it? After five years at rest Martha Anne Duffy was now at large. And missing.

He looks at the femur in his hand.

Well most of her was, anyway. And the question was: Who took her? It was a baffling case that would set in motion a chain of events so horrifying and...but I'm getting ahead of myself. For now, I just had to use my lifetime of detective experience and leave no clue unturned. Hello. What's this?

He glances at the ground.

Someone's dropped their library card. Best leave it here, they'll be back for it, I'm sure.

He walks off.

The kitchen of the Duffy farmhouse

There is a proliferation of cannabis plants around the room.

GERRY DUFFY is sitting, plucking at on old guitar, picking out a random series of notes trying to write a song.

GERRY *(crooning)* Linda...the German word for small child is kinder... Oh why does nothing really rhyme with... Linda... Even McCartney couldn't find a rhyme for... Linda...

He hears a noise from outside. Immediately he rises and grabs the poker.

Who is it? Who's there? I'm armed!

CLOUT *(outside)* No need for unpleasantness sir. It's the police. Detective Inspector Clout.

GERRY lowers the poker. He realises he has to hide the cannabis plants and starts hurriedly putting them into cupboards.

(Outside) Can I come in?

GERRY No! Wait there a moment, Inspector. I have to disable the bucket.

CLOUT *(outside)* Bucket, sir?

GERRY It's above the door. Intruder alert.

CLOUT *(outside)* Of course. Very ingenious.

GERRY has hidden all the plants except the last one on the table. At a loss, he drapes a tea towel over it.

(Outside) Will you be long?

GERRY Coming, Inspector.

GERRY *rushes out – a moment later he returns with* CLOUT, *who is holding an evidence bag.*

Sorry to keep you waiting.

CLOUT Don't you worry sir. I applaud your efforts. Crude but effective. Although, I couldn't help noticing your front gate is hanging off its hinges.

GERRY I haven't had it fixed since the last parcel bomb. Every time I call a carpenter to come and repair it, they think it's another hoax.

CLOUT You should complain.

GERRY I've tried. But your station ignores my calls for the same reason.

CLOUT Well, you can't blame the police for that. We're overstretched as it is, without responding to suspected hoax calls.

GERRY But what kind of hoax caller would ring up complaining about hoax calls?

CLOUT One with a social conscience? Who knows what goes on in these people's minds.

GERRY So who can I complain to?

CLOUT You're complaining to me, aren't you. And it's the right to constantly complain that proves we still live in the best country in the world. You should try fixing it yourself.

GERRY I don't get much time these days. I've spent all morning up a ladder, cleaning the side of the barn. Expunging the words "Fuck Scum Nazi Animal Killing Shitters".

CLOUT They're still doing that, are they? No sense of grammar, these people. Still, fret not, sir. We'll catch them one of these days.

GERRY You still believe that, do you? It's been three years since I last opened the curtains here?

CLOUT We're doing everything we possibly can.

GERRY Thirty-six months I've lived cowering.

CLOUT I just haven't got the resources.

GERRY One hundred and fifty-six weeks, checking beneath my car and over my shoulder every time I step out.

CLOUT They say it's a local matter.

GERRY One thousand and ninety-two days of exploding front gates and shite in the mail.

CLOUT Look on the bright side. It's done wonders for your mental arithmetic. I'm sorry, sir, but we can't arrest just anyone we like, you know. These probably aren't even foreigners we're dealing with here. In fact, judging by the state of their grammar and spelling, they were probably schooled locally.

GERRY Then forgive my asking, Inspector, but just what are you doing here?

CLOUT There have been developments.

GERRY What's happened?

CLOUT I'm not at liberty to disclose them as yet. But what I can tell you is I have been expecting something. However the something I've been expecting I certainly never expected to be something like this something. This something is totally unexpected. It's also very much a family matter, so I'll reveal all when your brother arrives.

GERRY Roger? Here? You'll be lucky, Inspector. He hasn't been near this place since Mother died.

Outside a bucket of water falls.

ROGER *offstage yells.*

CLOUT Yes, that's very effective, isn't it.

ROGER *enters. He is soaked and holds the bucket.*

ROGER What bloody maniac left this up there?

CLOUT Basic home security system, sir, courtesy of your brother.

ROGER What the hell's he doing here?

> ROGER *picks up the tea towel to dry himself. As he does,*
> GERRY *grabs the bucket and re-covers the cannabis plant.*

I came as soon as I got your message, Inspector but...

CLOUT But?

ROGER Well, I'm no doctor but my brother does appear to be a lot less dead than I was expecting.

CLOUT You were expecting him to be dead?

ROGER One lives in hope. You said something had happened to my brother.

CLOUT No, I said it was your mother.

ROGER Mother?

CLOUT Mother.

GERRY Mother?

CLOUT Mother.

GERRY Mother? She's dead and buried.

CLOUT Well, since last night you're fifty per cent correct.

GERRY What?

CLOUT I'm afraid they've dug her up.

ROGER Dug her up? What does that mean, "Dug her up"?

CLOUT It means she's been exhumed. Disinterred, uncovered, unburied and raised up.

GERRY She's been dug up?

CLOUT Exactly.

ROGER You're joking.

CLOUT I'm afraid I can't offer the irrational refuge of humour in this case.

GERRY "The irrational refuge of humour"? Do they teach you to speak like that in police school?

CLOUT I deal in facts and the facts are that yesterday morning your mother was dearly departed...

GERRY They must do.

CLOUT ...whereas this morning she made a bit of a comeback.

ROGER How low can these people get?

CLOUT Six feet apparently. However, we mustn't jump to conclusions as to the perpetrators of this foul desecration.

GERRY Just speak normally!

CLOUT The matter is still under investigation.

GERRY Well, who else could have dug her up? A renegade band of archaeologists? Or do you think she's risen from the grave?

ROGER Like the Resurrection?

GERRY I was thinking more of Night of the Living Dead. But either way it's not very likely is it Inspector? So, why can't you go out and do something?

ROGER Yes. Arrest these bloody animal rights...vegetarians.

CLOUT Vegetarianism isn't a crime. According my wife, it's a lifestyle choice.

ROGER So is being a criminal. And these days even they have rights.

CLOUT Everyone has rights.

ROGER But some people shouldn't have rights. They should lose the right to their rights.

GERRY But have you got the right to suppress their rights?

ROGER Oh don't you start. *I'm* not suppressing anyone. That's what I pay the police to do.

CLOUT Gentlemen, my hands are tied. If I call for help they tell me it's just a little local difficulty. Irate vegetarians aren't a national policing priority. Not like the war on terror. Or drugs.

CLOUT *picks up the bucket to make room for the evidence bag. He sees the cannabis.*

GERRY It's a tomato plant.

CLOUT Really? I'll take a cutting of that for my wife, if it's alright with you. She's quite the horticulturist these days. No, if these animal rights people were bona fide terrorists then I could use the new Emergency State Security Measures.

GERRY What are they then?

CLOUT No idea. They keep changing but they're always good. You give me a suspect and I can pick them up, lock them in, kick them out, you name it. You can get away with murder if you're safeguarding freedom.

GERRY That's a police state.

CLOUT I could have you in a strip cell for thirty days, begging for mercy for making such a dangerous suggestion.

GERRY But it's my right to oppose the system.

CLOUT That sounds to me like a "grave, exceptional threat". I could probably have you in for forty two days for that.

GERRY What happened to our civil liberties?

CLOUT We gave them up in order to safeguard them.

ROGER What's happened to this country?

CLOUT Now, that sounds suspiciously like a philosophical enquiry to me.

ROGER It is.

CLOUT The first rule of police work. Never stray into the realms of conceptual thought. It only leads to disquiet, unrest and convictions being overturned on appeal.

ROGER   Do you honestly think you can get a conviction, Inspector?

CLOUT   Not really, sir. There's not much point in this case. Desecration? It's just a slap on the wrists. First offence, previous good character, they'd claim they'd been influenced by something they'd seen on television.

ROGER   Like a video nasty?

CLOUT   Or Time Team. It doesn't really matter. By the time the social workers and bleeding heart do-gooders have finished, they'll be suing your old mum for damages to their spades.

ROGER   And they call this a land fit for heroes.

GERRY   No they don't.

CLOUT   But...

ROGER   There's a but?

CLOUT   There is a but. If they try to blackmail you for the return of her bones, then we've got them.

ROGER   Really, Inspector.

CLOUT   Oh yes. Because in law, we protect the pennies and not the dead man's eyes.

GERRY   What law is that, then? The Pennies and Dead Man's Eyes Act, 1968? Do you have a booklet with all this shit written in it?

CLOUT   Calm down Mr Duffy.

GERRY   Calm down! What is there to be calm about? I spend my life rubbing out graffiti while you're doing...what the fuck are you doing?! If we are going to have a police state can you at least organise it properly!

CLOUT   I'm doing my job, sir.

GERRY   Here we go. Another quote from the Midsomer Murder book of clichés.

CLOUT Wait long enough and the criminal will always make a fatal mistake.

GERRY What did I tell you!

CLOUT We have a lead. This.

With a flourish, CLOUT *takes the femur from the bag.*

GERRY What the hell's that?

CLOUT A femur. A thigh bone.

ROGER You don't mean it's...

CLOUT Yes. In their haste, they left it behind in the grave. And your mother's thighbone could turn out to be their Achilles heel.

ROGER Inspector, will you please stop waving my dead mother's thighs around.

CLOUT Now, I've only got the one.

GERRY And that makes it better?

CLOUT We must assume they are holding the other one. And I'll stake my professional reputation they'll be back to claim it.

ROGER Suddenly you've got a professional reputation?

CLOUT Which is why I'd like to leave it here. As bait.

GERRY And just what is our rationale for keeping bits of our dead mother around the place? Something to remember her by?

CLOUT Why not?

GERRY Why not. Because it's warped, that's why not.

ROGER And anyway, what makes you so sure they'll be back for it?

CLOUT Because what we're dealing with here is a highly dedicated and professionally minded group.

ROGER Of twisted loonies.

CLOUT They've managed to evade capture, which means they may be loonies but they're well organised. And I admire that in a loony.

ROGER You're very easily impressed, Inspector.

CLOUT So, any objections?

CLOUT *lays the femur on the table.*

GERRY Any point?

CLOUT Not really. I'll see myself out.

He turns and leaves.

GERRY *and* **ROGER** *look at the femur on the table.*

ROGER You could say it's nice to see me.

GERRY I could also say it's nice to have our dead mother's thighbone sitting on the kitchen table.

ROGER We have to give in to them now, you know.

GERRY Over my dead body.

ROGER Gerry, it's not your dead body we're talking about. Face reality.

GERRY That sounds like a remarkably defeatist attitude. Besides, I have my dignity.

ROGER Dignity?

GERRY Dignity.

ROGER Gerry, you're a frog farmer. This is a frog farm where you farm frogs. In terms of farming dignity it's up there with the production of rude-shaped vegetables.

GERRY It's the family business.

ROGER Gerry, look at the family and look at the business. Vivisection is dying. The golden age of psychopathic schoolboys slicing their way through millions of frogs in the name of O Level science is long past. Amphibian dissection is no longer necessary for modern life. If teenagers want to wield knives these days they can do it on each other.

GERRY I know. And that's why I've diversified.

ROGER Diversified?

GERRY Voila.

He holds up the cannabis plant.

Cannabis Sativa. Subspecies Indica. AKA dope, blow, Mary Jane, ganja, pot, hash, draw, skunk or, my own brand, toad.

ROGER And that's it, is it? Half a dozen weedy pot plants. That's what the "family business" has become? Look at you. Cowering. Huddled in this one room. The house closed up and shuttered against the world. You're living in darkness.

GERRY Come with me, brother.

GERRY *rises and puts on a pair of very dark glasses as he walks across to an interior door.* ROGER *follows him.* GERRY *unlocks the door and opens it. A shaft of brilliant light dazzles them.*

ROGER What the hell...

GERRY Hydroponic cultivation. Ten thousand plants under high pressure sodium lamps for optimum photosynthesis. That's why I live in here. I'm not a great sleeper at the best of times but a constant fifty thousand lumens is guaranteed to give anyone nightmares.

ROGER If the police found this lot...

GERRY I'd say it was for my rheumatism.

ROGER You don't have rheumatism.

GERRY So it obviously works. Anyway, for the law to find it would take Detective Inspector Clout to actually solve a case.

ROGER But what if someone else found out?

GERRY Like who? I don't get any visitors. And I haven't told anyone.

ROGER You've told me.

GERRY It's your farm too, brother. Remember?

ROGER So the frogs are just a front?

GERRY Sort of. Remember what Dad always said was the secret of a successful business?

ROGER Avoid tax and fuck the other bloke over?

GERRY The other thing. Synergy. Get the two sides of the business working hand in hand. Or, in this case, hand in flipper.

ROGER Frogs and dope?

GERRY Not frogs. Come on, Roger. You were always the swot. The one who knows all there is to know about frogs and...

ROGER Toads? Not... Bufo Marinus.

GERRY Right in one!

ROGER Cane toads!

GERRY Don't knock it. I tell you, this stuff, infused with essence of cane toad...the kids are mad for it.

ROGER Mad? They'll be bloody psychotic!

GERRY It's just a bit of fun! Do you know, there have been less recorded deaths from smoking cane toad soaked cannabis than there have from...lots of other things. And maybe it's what kids today need to open their mind to what is going on in the world.

ROGER They smoke this stuff and all that will be going on in their world is hallucinations, paranoia and insanity.

GERRY I see you're still reading the Daily Mail.

ROGER They'll lock you up for life.

GERRY There's no risk. All done on the net.

ROGER I might have known, The bloody internet. The great technological miracle. Ninety five per cent pornography and now five per cent cane toad saturated drugs. Gerry...

GERRY I'm not selling, Roger.

He walks through the light into the room.

ROGER Gerry. Gerry...

ROGER *follows him into the light – as* **CLOUT** *walks out, addressing the audience.*

CLOUT So this is what I was facing. A missing person, answering to the description "Skeletal", a farm under siege and a potential terrorist plot. It was my belief they were all somehow connected. And it was my job to find out how.

The door shuts, leaving him in darkness.

Jago's flat

A sack containing the bones sits on the coffee table.

Two muddied spades lean against the wall.

MARC *enters. He is agitated. Pacing.*

MARC Jago? ...Jago.

JAGO *enters, pressing a towel to his neck.*

JAGO What?

MARC Jago. Last night. We didn't do what I think we did, did we?

JAGO Do you mean, did we strike a bold, decisive and historic blow for the liberation of animal kind?

MARC That wasn't quite how I was going to put it.

JAGO Well you should. Because we did.

MARC Oh Christ!

JAGO Why else did you join the movement?

MARC I joined because I thought... I believe we shouldn't be nasty to animals.

JAGO Is that it, is it? That's your manifesto? Your revolutionary philosophical credo. "We shouldn't be nasty to animals".

MARC All right. We *definitely* shouldn't be nasty to animals. In fact, we should be nice to them.

JAGO And why's that, then?

MARC Why's what, then?

JAGO Why should we be not nasty and in fact "definitely nice" to the poor little fluffy animals.

MARC You mean you don't know?

JAGO I know.

MARC And so do I. It's... It's because it's not their fault they're
animals.

JAGO *(in disgust)* Oh, for fuck's sake!

MARC No. Listen, right, okay. When I was eight, right, I went
to work with my dad. It was really exciting. I remember it.
Day off school, with Dad. I knew he worked with animals.
I always thought he was a vet. Turned out he was a slaughter
man. It really spoiled my day. Because his job was to hold
the bolt still while his mate, my uncle Simon, smacked it
into the forehead of the cows. Cow after cow after cow after
cow. They were like animals. But it wasn't their fault. It's
just what they did. Then, on the way home, he took me for
a Happy Meal as a treat. But I couldn't face it. And that's
when I knew. That day when I was eight years old. But...

JAGO But?

MARC But I don't know... I somehow always thought I could
do it by adopting a panda or something.

JAGO *(shocked)* Adopting a panda?! What kind of human
arrogance is this? Suddenly you know best how to raise a
panda, do you? Better than its natural mother.

MARC No. I was just saying...

JAGO You think you can suckle a cub, do you? Forage for
bamboo? Raise a tiny little panda cub into consciousness
of its proud but endangered heritage?

MARC No! Alright! Forget the panda idea. I don't know, maybe
I could work in a vegan wholefood shop or something.

JAGO And that's your idea of commitment to the cause of animal
liberation. Pandas and tofu.

MARC I said forget the panda! Look Jago, I'm trying to work
out what's happened. What we've done. How I got from

wanting to be nice to cows to digging up old ladies. What gives us the right to do this?

JAGO The "right"?

MARC Yes.

JAGO Another human concept that's up there with panda adoption. We haven't got the "right" to do it. We haven't got the "right" to do anything.

MARC But in that case...

JAGO We're on the side of the animals, yes?

MARC Yes.

JAGO And do animals have rights?

MARC Yes.

JAGO No.

MARC Don't they?

JAGO No. Because we "humans" haven't given them any.

MARC Right. And that's why we're fighting. To give rights to animals. Yes?

JAGO No. Because what right do we have to give them rights? The very idea pre-supposes that it is human beings who are the superior species.

MARC Which means...

JAGO Which means, we're on the side of the animals, right? Animals don't have any rights, which means animals can't be wrong, right? Ipso facto, we can do what the fuck we want. Am I wrong or am I right? Marc, we are going to free every animal in the world. Even the animals who are free are going to be more free thanks to us.

MARC Really?

JAGO And we start by making those bastards close that torture farm of theirs. We are going to make them suffer.

MARC Until they agree to embrace a cruelty-free lifestyle?

JAGO Exactly.

MARC Okay. So what are we going to do with her?

JAGO Who?

MARC Her.

JAGO The bones?

MARC Yes. I'm not sharing the flat with her.

JAGO But she's quiet, good sense of humour. And she wasn't cremated and so she's a non-smoker.

MARC But she's evidence! Incriminating evidence. What if someone comes round?

JAGO Now there, you make a good point. We'll have to bury her.

MARC But we've only just dug her up.

> JAGO *picks up a spade and holds it out to* MARC.

JAGO Find somewhere quiet, out of the way. Okay?

MARC Me?

JAGO Of course you. I've got things to do.

MARC What things?

JAGO Leadership things.

MARC Such as?

JAGO Such as? Listen, a concentrated campaign of intimidation and violence against the status quo takes planning. Management. You can't just smash the system willy-nilly. That would be anarchy. Marc, this is your moment.

> MARC *reluctantly accepts the spade.*

MARC Okay. And you're going to do your leadership things?

JAGO I'm going to work out how to establish communications with the enemy.

MARC You're going to phone them?

JAGO Yes! I'm going to phone them! The struggle never ends until the frogs are free!

JAGO's *voice echoes around the village.*

The graveyard

CLOUT *is standing at the graveside.*

CLOUT *(hearing the voice)* "Until the frogs are free"? *(To audience)* Did you hear that?

He gets out his notebook, notes it down and wanders off in search of the voice.

The kitchen of the Duffy farmhouse

The curtains are closed and GERRY *is sitting at the table, cutting, weighing and packing cannabis using scales and a knife.*

GERRY *(singing confidently)*
LINDA...

There is a long pause as he thinks. Then shrugs.

Fuck it.

Beside him in a little tank is a cane toad. GERRY *picks it up.*

(To the frog) Why couldn't she have been called... I don't know... Joan? *(He sings)*

JOAN, OH JOANIE... MY DEAD MUM'S LEG, IT LOOKS SO BONY.

GERRY *gently rolls cannabis resin over the toad.*

Now...come on little feller...that's right...squeeze it out for Daddy... That's lovely...well done...

GERRY *carefully puts the resin down but before he returns the toad to its tank he tries to resist but fails and gives it a big, sensuously hungry lick.*

Ooooh boy.

The toad goes back in the tank and GERRY *turns what is left of his attention back to cutting and weighing the resin.*

After a few seconds the interior door opens.

White light shafts into the room.

Through the light TWO FROGS *enter (played by the actors who play* JAGO *and* MARC*). They both wear white lab coats. One of them carries a clipboard.*

All right, lads? How's it going? I tell you, it's been quite busy round here. *(Waves femur at them)* Have you met Mum? I've had the police round. And my brother. Unfortunately he's more real than you two...but only just. So, what's the topic of conversation for today? And, if it's okay with you, do you think we could possibly have something slightly less frog-related for a change? I mean, I'm not criticising or anything, it's just I've noticed all we ever seem to talk about these days is...well...frogs. And froggy things.

The FROGS *come and stand either side of him, looking him over critically.* FROG 2 *makes the occasional note.*

(Unsettled by their manner) Don't take it personally or anything. It's just that given you are like my own imaginary little green friends, and theoretically, I am in control of you, I was thinking maybe we could talk about me for once.

FROG 1 *(interrupting)* And you say its central nervous system is similar to our own?

FROG 2 Well, similarish.

FROG 1 Similarish? What does that mean exactly?

FROG 2 Exactly? Well, it means 'sort of'. "Close enough".

GERRY Hello? Guys?

FROG 2 Of course the thing is, though, we're not really going to know until we rip it open and have a good old look inside.

FROG 1 No, I suppose not.

GERRY Have I done something to upset you?

FROG 2 But the point is, it does have a central nervous system.

GERRY Okay. Let's talk frogs. I just thought, for a change, maybe...

FROG 2 It can feel pain. Look.

FROG 2 *produces a long needle and pricks* GERRY.

GERRY Ow! What did you do that for?

FROG 2 See.

FROG 1 Interesting.

FROG 2 Isn't it.

GERRY I'm sorry? What's so interesting about that? Prick me and I bleed.

FROG 2 *pricks* GERRY *again.*

Ow! I didn't mean it literally! What's wrong with you two today?

FROG 1 From that, I'll grant you, that it does appear to experience something similar to what we recognise as pain.

FROG 2 Surely...

FROG 2 *plunges the needle back into* GERRY.

GERRY Ow!!!

FROG 2 ...is more than an appearance of pain.

GERRY OK! Enough! Look, you two, I don't mind you visiting, which is just as well as I don't seem to be able to stop you. And even though you are six-foot frogs, I'm man enough to admit there have been times when I've been glad of your company. But please! There's no need to suddenly turn nasty, is there.

FROG 1 But that very observation leads us to the question, should we be doing this?

FROG 2 Doing what?

FROG 1 Tormenting this poor creature in this way.

GERRY Yes. Good point.

FROG 2 This isn't torment. It's science. This is how we advance as a species.

FROG 1 But doesn't this thing have a God-given right to...you know...

GERRY Not be stabbed to death.

FROG 2 What are you talking about? Rights aren't "God-given". They're frog given. And we haven't given it any.

GERRY Oh shit!

FROG 2 And besides we haven't established empirically if it even feels pain.

GERRY Trust me guys, I do. So come on. Who was your favourite Muppet?

FROG 1 I suppose the problem is, we need some categorical assurance that the experience of pain is universal.

FROG 2 Exactly. So let's cut him open then. It'll be best for him in the long run.

FROG 1 Oh, very well.

The FROGS grab the protesting GERRY and wrestle him to the floor.

Before they can disembowel him the telephone rings.

The FROGS immediately run back through the interior door, which slams shut behind them.

Dazed and confused, GERRY scrabbles to the phone and answers it.

GERRY Hello?

We hear JAGO's distorted voice on the other end of the line.

JAGO Where's Mamma gone? Wouldn't you like to know. You want Mummy back? Then you know what you have to do. Because you know this is never going to stop until you do it, don't you... Don't you! Say...

GERRY Yes. I know.

JAGO Then you know what to do. Don't you?

GERRY Yes.

JAGO And remember, we're watching you. We're close.

JAGO hangs up.

GERRY hears a noise outside and in terror he grabs the poker.

Outside the bucket crashes down on Roger who yells.

GERRY throws open the curtains and dives out through the window.

CARO and ROGER enter. ROGER is wet and carrying the bucket.

ROGER Why doesn't he just get a bloody burglar alarm?

CARO *(calling)* Uncle Gerry!

CARO goes to open the interior door. ROGER quickly bars her way.

ROGER He won't be in there! He only lives in this room. Spends all his time in here. The rest of the house is...booby trapped. It's like a minefield.

CARO What he's had to put with all this time. A lesser man would have cracked.

ROGER Caroline, your uncle is a lesser man and he has cracked. Many times.

CARO So we have to help him. The last three years must have been hell for him. And now...this. When is this nightmare going to stop?

ROGER I just don't know, sweetheart.

CARO You have to know. It's up to us. We have to do whatever it takes to get Granny back. Sell this place. Close it down. Burn it to the ground. Anything they demand.

ROGER Right now there's nothing I'd like more. But it's not that easy. You know half of it belongs to your uncle. I can't do anything without his agreement. And he won't see sense.

CARO But he must. This place is a House of Death. I live in the real world.

ROGER You live in St Neots.

CARO Yes, and I'm doing bloody nicely there, thank you. And what I *don't* need is being constantly reminded that I'm related to the fucking Addams Family. We've got to make Uncle Gerry live in the real world with us.

ROGER You want him in St Neots?

CARO No. Okay, so we don't want him in *our* real world. But he can't stay here. You don't know what these people are capable of. They might kidnap one of us!

ROGER They wouldn't.

CARO They might. And then they could do something really terrible. Like...

ROGER Like what?

CARO Like...bury us alive.

ROGER No.

CARO How do you know?

ROGER Because it makes no sense. And these people may be maniacs but they're not mad.

CARO Not mad? They've dug up someone who's dead. Surely that's more mad than burying someone who's alive. Because if they bury someone who's alive and you and Uncle Gerry don't sell the farm quick enough, whoever they've buried alive will die. Then when they're dead, they'll dig them up again and we'll be back where we started!

ROGER There, there, darling. You're upsetting yourself.

CARO Of course I am. This is my granny we're talking about. And I loved her. Even if you didn't.

ROGER Caroline. That's not fair. I've never said I didn't love Granny.

CARO But you didn't. Oh Daddy.

ROGER You know, darling girl, sometimes I think you're the only person I'd care about enough to dig up if you were buried alive by maniacs.

CARO That's sweet. Now just promise me you'll do whatever it takes to get Granny returned to us.

ROGER I promise.

CARO Because if you don't then...then *I'll* do something.

ROGER Like what?

CARO I don't know. I might harm myself.

ROGER Again? I'm not sure that will stop them.

CARO It always works with you.

ROGER I promise. I'll talk to your uncle.

CARO I know you can get through to him. Deep down he's a reasonable man.

GERRY bursts through the door. He is in the grip of a psychotic episode. He's brandishing the poker.

GERRY Where are they? Where are they!? The nasty, vicious green bastards!

ROGER Gerry! What are you talking about?

GERRY The six-foot frogs. I know they're around here somewhere.

He rushes out again.

ROGER Er...leave it with me, darling. I'll just have a little word with him.

CARO *(screams)*

ROGER What!? A long word?

CARO What the hell is that bone?

ROGER That? It's Granny's thigh, of course.

CARO They left it behind?

ROGER Yes...

GERRY *(offstage)* Eugh!!! Green! Green! Keep your nasty flippers off me...

ROGER Er...could you just give me a moment, my love? Just need to...don't start...doing anything to yourself. I'll be right back. *(Leaving after* **GERRY***)* Gerry? Have you got a minute. Just want a quick word.

CARO *picks up the femur.*

CARO I don't believe this.

GERRY *bursts back in.*

GERRY Kermit was a wanker!

He rushes out again followed by **CARO**.

The graveyard

CLOUT *is standing at the graveside.*

CLOUT Kermit may well have been a wanker, but that wasn't what was bothering me. Now, of course, if I'd have known back then what I came to know later...then I'd have been Miss bloody Marple! Because it's all very well for detectives on the telly. Nice little murder. Five suspects, four motives and all you have to do is nick the one who looks most like Nigel Havers. But this... Well, believe it or not, *this* was real bloody life. And Nigel Havers doesn't live round these parts.

Jago's flat

JAGO, *wearing his frog mask, is sitting in front of an old video camera.*

JAGO ...The immediate end to the use of non-human animals for food, clothing, research or entertainment... *(Takes a toke)* ...Twenty Seventhly, Colonel Sanders to be indicted for war crimes...

MARC *enters.*

MARC Jago?

JAGO Get out of the back of the shot! And don't use my name, Marc.

MARC What are you doing?

JAGO The ransom video.

MARC On VHS? It's a bit eighties, isn't it. It's got to be on DVD now, at least.

JAGO What?

MARC Or a simple download. Mpeg it over to them.

JAGO Bin Laden always used video.

MARC He was in a cave in Afghanistan. They've probably still got Betamax over there. But these days, ISIS, they've got their own hi-def YouTube channel. You want to set up a webcam or something.

JAGO *tears off his mask in frustration.*

JAGO Marc, we're not a fucking I.T. department! You can't smash the human machine on Twitter.

MARC I'm just saying...

JAGO What? What are you "just saying".

MARC I'm just saying they probably haven't got a video player. Before they can submit to our demands they'll have to get them transferred to a compatible format.

JAGO Right! Fine! I'll write them on a piece of paper, then shall I?

MARC It might be quicker.

JAGO So where did you put it?

MARC What?

JAGO Her.

MARC Who?

JAGO The bones!

MARC Them.

JAGO Yes.

MARC In the woods.

JAGO The woods! Everyone's there walking their dogs.

MARC No one saw me.

JAGO They'd better not. You might have to move her again.

MARC Oh no. I dug her up last night, I've buried her again today. If she's moving again, you're doing it.

JAGO I'm not doing it. I'm the leader.

MARC Oh, stop being so pig-headed.

JAGO Pig-headed? I'm "pig-headed" am I?

MARC Yes. You are.

JAGO Well, I happen to think that pigs have beautiful heads.

MARC You know what I mean.

JAGO I know you're using the idea of a pig's head as a term of abuse for human beings. Which I find both speciesist and degrading to pigs.

MARC Speciesist? Is that one of yours?

JAGO The fact that there's no better word for speciesism than speciesist, is typical of human prejudice against other species.

MARC It is one of yours.

JAGO The head of a pig could never be filled with the cruelty and self-interest that fill a human's... Marc.

MARC You haven't got many friends, have you.

> **JAGO** *starts scribbling demands on a pad.*

> *They hear a sound from someone outside.*

JAGO Who's that?

MARC I don't know.

JAGO You were followed! Someone saw you! Hide the spade!

> *The door opens, revealing* **CARO**. *She is holding the femur.*

CARO I don't believe this.

MARC It was his idea. He made me.

CARO Well, Graham?

MARC Graham?

CARO What have you done?

MARC Graham?

JAGO Leave it, Marc. Caro, we have struck a blow at the forces of...speciesism and taken decisive action to help free the oppressed and enslaved.

CARO So you haven't just dug up my granny, then?

JAGO Don't personalise this, Caro.

MARC Although we do understand that the digging up of close relations could be construed as being a pretty personal matter.

JAGO Caro, this is not the time for weak sentimentality. You must decide where you stand. Oppression and brutality – or frogs. There's nothing in between.

MARC But Graham...

JAGO Jago! My name's Jago. Okay?

MARC Okay. Jago. Caro didn't ask to be born into a family of frog murderers and I think she has every right to be shocked and upset by this monstrous outrage we have committed. For the best of reasons. And which we didn't, in any way, enjoy. Did we, Jago?

JAGO remains silent.

We found the whole experience highly traumatising. We realise we crossed a line. Went too far. We didn't know what we were doing. We were misguided and cruel and... I'm sorry!!! God! *I'm so sorry!* Caro!!! Forgive me! Forgive me!!!

CARO I think...it's genius!

MARC You do?

JAGO As he said, I made him do it.

MARC But it's your granny.

CARO You never knew the old bitch. I did. And trust me, my grandmother was a woman immeasurably improved by death. So yes, I say it's genius...in every respect but one.

JAGO What?

CARO You two idiots managed to leave a bit of her behind.

MARC Of her...behind?

CARO Her thighbone. But hopefully they're finally going to see sense.

MARC They're going to close the farm?

CARO And sell the land!

JAGO They've agreed?

CARO Not yet. But they will. I've made my father promise me.

MARC How can you trust him?

CARO My father always gives me everything I want. It's why I feel so deprived.

JAGO Any agreement on the decommissioning of the Japanese whaling fleet?

CARO We didn't really get into it.

MARC Still, they're going to close the farm.

CARO And sell the land!

MARC *(meaningfully)* Close the farm. You know what this means.

CARO For the frogs?

MARC For us. Remember what you said?

CARO Of course I do, darling. But as I told you, I can't think of having an "us" until all this is over and my awful family have atoned for what they've done.

MARC Oh, my poor darling.

CARO I can't think of myself as worthy of anyone's love until I've made the nightmare stop.

MARC I don't mind. Honestly.

He makes to kiss her but she moves away.

CARO No. I can't. Not whilst that terrible place is still open. Every time I look at you all I see is the tormented face of a pathetic, defeated little frog screaming back at me.

MARC That's not good, is it.

CARO It's a bit off-putting.

MARC But the farm's as good as closed.

CARO As good as. But not completely.

MARC Right. And you couldn't manage a quickie until...

CARO No.

MARC *(resigned)* No.

CARO But every moment brings the final victory closer. Emancipation is at hand, thanks to you. You've been so... wonderful. So where is she?

MARC Who?

CARO Granny?

MARC I've buried her.

CARO But you'd only just dug her up.

MARC I know but he told me to.

CARO Well, now that Daddy's going to get Uncle Gerry to agree to selling the farm, they're going to want her back. So we'll have to dig her up again.

JAGO Agreed. Off you go, Marc.

MARC Me?

JAGO Of course you. You're the only one who knows where you buried her.

MARC But I could tell you where she is and you could do it?

JAGO You can't tell *anyone* where she is. The whole operation relies on top secrecy.

CARO Marc...darling...please, without the bones they'll never close the farm. And without the farm closed, there's no us.

MARC *(realising he's beaten)* Oh...all right.

He rises.

CARO And whilst you're out, check the grave.

MARC What for?

CARO You left her thigh bone in there, God knows what else you might have left. Just check it.

MARC But...

CARO Remember, you're doing it for the cause. For the third emancipation. First it was the slaves, then it was women. Now it's the turn of the frogs. Don't let them down. Do it for them.

MARC And for us.

CARO Yes, that too.

MARC just sighs and leaves.

CARO and JAGO sit in awkward silence. They hear the front door bang shut. They wait for two beats and then leap on each other.

Yes! God, I'm brilliant.

JAGO I know. What a genius idea. Dig up your own granny.

CARO I know.

They start tearing at each other's clothes.

She pushes his head down between her breasts.

The front door bangs shut again.

They freeze and then immediately roll apart and sit upright.

MARC I forgot the shovel.

He sees CARO and JAGO's dishevelled clothing.

What's happened?

JAGO What's happened? What's happened, Marc? I'll tell you what's happened, shall I? You, Marc, you have forgotten the shovel. *That's* what's happened. And *that's* the sort of sloppiness that's compromising this whole operation, Marc.

MARC No, I meant...

JAGO Don't change the subject, Marc. We all have our roles to play. Keep focused.

JAGO *picks up the shovel and thrusts it at* MARC.

Don't forget the shovel.

MARC *(to* CARO*)* Are you okay, darling?

CARO I'm fine. Darling. But Jago's right. You have to do your bit.

JAGO And we'll do ours.

CARO Yes. For us.

JAGO And the frogs. And by the way...

JAGO *tears the page of demands from the pad.*

...these are our demands to the authorities.

JAGO *wraps them around a house brick which he hands to* MARC.

Drop them off on your way.

MARC Isn't that your job?

JAGO Yes. But if you're passing...

MARC Okay. I'll see you later then.

MARC *takes the shovel and leaves.*

CARO *and* JAGO *sit back on the sofa.*

The front door bangs shut.

They sit. They wait. Their breathing gets heavier.

JAGO If we do it doggy fashion...

CARO Yes?

JAGO Is that demeaning to dogs or women? Or both?

CARO Want to find out?

JAGO You bet.

CARO And Jago, I know you're a vegan...

She pushes his head down between her legs.

...but I want you to eat *this*!

CARO*'s voice echoes around the village.*

The graveyard

CLOUT *is pointlessly measuring the grave. He hears* CARO's *echoing voice. He quickly makes a note in his book then takes out his phone and dials.*

CLOUT PC Cox? ...Have you got a pen? Take this down. "Until the frogs are free... I want you to eat this." ...No, I don't know what it means, but it's all we've got to go on...just write it down!

He turns off the phone.

(To audience) It's obviously code of some sort. But so far the investigation was progressing exactly as I predicted. Totally unpredictably. But, the case was about to be blown wide open.

The kitchen of the Duffy farmhouse

ROGER *is sitting at the table.*

GERRY *is obsessively picking out the same notes (from the Linda song) over and over on his guitar.*

GERRY *(crooning)* The ancient Greek poet... Pinder... Was looking through the...winder...

ROGER *(eventually)* You know, I always said you should have kept up with the music. Not the lyrics, obviously. Never been your thing.

GERRY You never said you liked my music.

ROGER Didn't I? I said it to Linda all the time. I never understood why you left the band.

GERRY It wasn't going anywhere.

ROGER Four UK top tens and a handful of European number ones.

GERRY I never sold out.

ROGER Gerry, you've never sold *in*. And now you just sit here, alone. *(Quickly)* Sorry! You're not alone. I forgot, you have two six-foot frogs for company. By the way, are they here now?

GERRY No they're not. Thank God. Because between you and me, they've started to go a bit odd.

ROGER Gerry, you have to get out of here. Sell this place and come into the business with me.

GERRY Your "Garden Centre"?

ROGER Oh, I know you've always sneered at it. Sneering is what you do best. But I've worked bloody hard at it. And I've built it up into something. Four retail outlets. Three more planned. It's a good, honest business.

GERRY Which employs people on "good, honest" zero-hours contracts.

ROGER Oh, spare me!

GERRY What about your workers' rights?

ROGER You know, brother, you spend so much of your life sitting on your backside, defending everyone else's rights that you don't realise that it's everyone's right to think they have the right to stop *us* having any rights.

GERRY It's an interesting philosophical point you make.

ROGER No! Don't tell me that!

GERRY Don't shout at me, Roger. It's not my fault that, after all these years, you've finally said something interesting.

ROGER It's not an "interesting philosophical point", you smug bastard. Can't you see? It's real life! As lived by every normal person in the world except you. It's what I wake up to every bloody morning. It's what I see staring back at me in the shaving mirror. And every bloody morning, I see there's a little bit less and a little bit less than there was the bloody morning before. Every day it's like I'm losing more and more and what I lose some other bastard gets!

GERRY Roger, I'm sorry, you were right. It wasn't an interesting philosophical point at all. It was rather dull and self-pitying. Thanks for the offer of joining you in your garden centre but if it's all the same to you, I'll stick where I am. I'm not sure my plants would fit in too well amongst the hydrangeas and yuccas.

ROGER For Christ's sake, Gerry, get real! These people are holding the remains of our mother hostage. If we don't do what they want, we'll never get her back.

GERRY Do we really want her back?

ROGER What kind of question's that? "Do we really want her back?"

GERRY But do we? Really? Look, we've buried her once, they've dug her up once. If we get her back and bury her again, how do we know she won't pop up again. She's our mother, not a hardy annual. We don't want to be planting her every spring. Much better to say, if you want her that much, you can have her?

ROGER How can you be so callous and unfeeling?

GERRY Personally, I've always blamed my mother. They think we want her back but what if we don't? They can have her. She's all theirs.

ROGER I don't understand.

GERRY Try thinking outside the box.

ROGER Poor choice of words. Gerry, she was our mother.

GERRY I know. And what would you do if she walked in through the door, right now?

ROGER Through the door? You mean alive and living and breathing and...back?

GERRY Yes.

ROGER Christ! Well, obviously I wouldn't want that. But as long as she's dead she has to be buried properly.

GERRY No she doesn't.

ROGER Yes she does.

GERRY I don't see why.

ROGER Of course you don't see why. It's alright for you. You didn't kill her. I did.

CLOUT enters. He carries a pole with the full bucket of water hooked on the end of it.

CLOUT Evening gentlemen. I'm not disturbing anything, am I?

ROGER No! Nothing at all.

CLOUT puts the bucket down on the table.

CLOUT I'm afraid I've found a loophole in your security system.

GERRY Is that why you came round?

CLOUT No, that's just a serendipitous consequence. I'm here for the cutting. The tomato plant. I forgot it the other day and Mrs Clout was very disappointed. Particularly after I described it to her, she's most anxious to try her hand at cultivation.

CLOUT *produces a pair of scissors.*

So, if it's alright with you.

GERRY *(quickly)* To tell you the truth, Inspector, it's not much of a tomato plant.

ROGER You can say that again.

CLOUT You mean you haven't had any toms off it?

GERRY Not one.

CLOUT Oh well, not to worry. I'm sure Mrs C will have more luck. She's very green fingered.

CLOUT *advances towards the plant.* ROGER *and* GERRY *look at each other hopelessly. But before* CLOUT *cuts it he stops.*

Where's the bone?

ROGER The bone?

CLOUT It was here. Bait. Remember?

GERRY It's gone.

CLOUT I can see it's gone, sir. Hence my question. It's a thighbone. It can't just walk off. Has anyone else been in here?

GERRY Apart from the six-foot frogs?

ROGER *(quickly)* Yes, thank you, Gerry. No one, Inspector.

CLOUT Hmm. Bit of a mystery, wouldn't you say.

CLOUT *turns his attention back to the cutting.*

Now...

The brick with JAGO's *demands wrapped around it flies through the window.*

ROGER What the hell was that?

GERRY The sort of thing you get used to living here. But you've got to admire the timing.

CLOUT *picks up the brick and looks over the demands.*

ROGER So what do they want?

GERRY Whatever it is we won't give in.

ROGER Yes we will!

CLOUT I can't help but admire their optimism. Although I do feel they may have overestimated the global impact of their high jinks. But the point is, now this is no longer just a little light-hearted grave robbery and desecration. Now this is terrorism.

GERRY That is such a comfort.

CLOUT It is to me. Because you are now a Police Budgetary Priority. I can throw a 24-hour ring of steel around this place. Nothing will get in or out.

GERRY Ring of steel?

CLOUT They won't get past us. Excuse me, I've got some national security to put into action.

CLOUT *takes out his phone and dials, walking downstage.*

GERRY Roger! What do you mean, you killed Mother? Are you sure?

ROGER Matricide isn't something that allows room for doubt.

CLOUT *(on phone)* PC Cox, it's me... Well, who did you think it was?

ROGER It was after Linda left. Or rather, after Linda decided that I should leave. I was back here.

GERRY I remember.

CLOUT *(on phone)* The situation has just moved to Defcon One.

ROGER Mother never liked Linda.

GERRY Mother never liked anyone.

CLOUT *(on phone)* Defcon One... It means... Bloody serious, is what it means.

ROGER But that night she was so...vicious and spiteful and...

GERRY Motherly?

ROGER After all the years of it, I'd had enough.

CLOUT *(on phone)* Defcon? I don't know, Toby, it's just a thing that means "bloody serious".

GERRY So what did you do?

ROGER I... I prayed.

GERRY You prayed?

ROGER To God. I got down on my knees and beseeched the Lord to strike down our own mother.

GERRY And that was it?

CLOUT *(on phone)* Well, how about, "Code Red". Is that better? ...Yes? ...Then it's Code Red here.

GERRY Roger, I know he's a terrible and vengeful God and all that, but I don't think he does contract hits.

ROGER You reckon? The next morning, Gerry, the very next morning, we found her. Remember? Sitting up in bed. Cold. We all said it was her time and that it was a merciful release...

GERRY It was for us.

ROGER But I knew. I knew what I'd done.

GERRY Jesus.

ROGER   And I've had to live with it every day since. Her, you, this house, a horrible, constant reminder. And then, when they called and I thought you were dead, it was like it was finally all over. I saw not just the light but the entire end of the tunnel rushing towards me. After all these years, the bright, blessed sunshine of a normal existence. I thought I could move on. But of course it was the lights of the Animals Rights Nutter Express hurtling straight towards me instead. Digging it all up. I need it buried again. It's why we have to get out of here.

CLOUT   *(on phone)* So, I want all available manpower up here now.

GERRY   I can't leave.

ROGER   But the police are going to be here.

GERRY   Exactly. I can't leave the police here...with...

ROGER   With what?

GERRY   The "tomato plants".

ROGER   Shit! We've got to get out of here!

     ROGER *makes for the door.*

CLOUT   *(on phone)* This is going to be an all-nighter. So get the overtime forms out... Top left-hand drawer.

GERRY   Roger calm down.

ROGER   There's nothing to be calm about. I've got to get out. I've got to get out.

     ROGER *climbs out of the window.*

CLOUT   *(on phone)* No, it's alright, Toby, I've got some sandwiches... Right. Ten four, over and out, see you soon.

     CLOUT *turns off the phone.*

Right, I'm locking this place down for the night, so...where's your brother gone?

GERRY Just popped out to look for a missing backbone.

GERRY *settles himself down at the table.*

CLOUT *runs a "security check" on the kitchen. He goes to try the interior door leading to the cannabis plants.* It's locked.

CLOUT I see.

GERRY Hasn't been opened in years.

CLOUT I see. And the key?

GERRY Lost.

CLOUT That's unfortunate. However, if it keeps the bloodthirsty hoard of maniacs from slaying us in our sleep tonight, then it will work to our advantage.

CLOUT *settles at the other end of the table.*

Don't you worry, sir. They can't get you now. It's going to be a long night.

The graveyard

A flashlight is shining up from inside the grave. There is a noise. The flashlight goes out and MARC's *head bobs up. He sees a figure approaching and bobs back into the grave.*

ROGER *enters. He is drunk and kneels at the graveside.*

ROGER Mother! Mother, who did this to you? Who did this to *us*? Who? Whose!? Who's library card is this?

He flings card away.

Oh, Mother. I'm sorry. I'm so very sorry. All my life, I've spent it blaming Gerry. But now, I see, finally, that I have been wrong. I can't blame my brother for the way my life's turned out. It's not *his* fault. It's *yours* Mother! It was always you! Thanks! Thank you, so very bloody, bleeding, sodding well much, Mum!

During this ROGER *has opened his flies and started peeing into the grave.*

Oh, that's better. If you were here now, Mum, what you say?

MARC For fuck's sake, stop pissing on me!

ROGER *screams and scrambles to his feet and in doing so falls into the grave.*

The kitchen of the Duffy farmhouse

CLOUT *and* GERRY *are at the table.* CLOUT *has a foil package of sandwiches. He offers one to* GERRY.

CLOUT Sandwich?

GERRY No thanks.

CLOUT No? I can't really blame you. Avocado, grape and rocket. I mean, I ask you. That's not a sandwich, is it. It's a random collection of words squashed between two bits of bread. What's happened to sandwiches these days?

Pause.

The problem is, it's Mrs Clout. She makes them for me. I think she thinks it's a nice thing to do. You've never married have you, sir?

GERRY No.

CLOUT No, of course you haven't. Not that it makes any difference. Not to me, anyway. Whether you are, whether you aren't, I don't mind. I'm not allowed to mind. Even you lot have rights these days. Apparently.

The interior door opens. The white light floods out and the two FROGS *enter.*

CLOUT *and the* FROGS *remain unaware of each other throughout this scene.*

GERRY *(sotto)* Not now! Not tonight. Please!

CLOUT But, I don't mind telling you, back when I joined up, it was all very different. Back then it was all very unenlightened. Quite shocking in many ways. A hippy poof like you wouldn't have lasted very long. No offence.

GERRY *(to the* FROGS*)* What's going on?

CLOUT Just what I ask myself, sometimes. I also ask Mrs Clout, but she's no help. She very much does her own thing these days. Like vegetarianism. She's coming up to that age. It'll be pottery and psychology classes next.

FROG 1 It appears agitated.

FROG 2 Yes. That is how it appears.

GERRY Inspector!

CLOUT Yes, sir? Changed your mind about the sandwich have you?

GERRY *(gesturing to a* **FROG***)* You...you can't see it, can you?

CLOUT Vegetarianism? No, no I can't sir. I don't want to eat this. I want a proper sandwich. Ham or cheese.

The **FROGS** *advance on* **GERRY***.*

GERRY What have I done to deserve this?

CLOUT My thoughts entirely.

FROG 2 But who knows what goes on in this creature?

CLOUT Still, I suppose you get what you're given.

FROG 2 When I stub my flipper against a rock, the sensation I feel I call"pain". You may call it "pleasure", "hunger" or "homesickness" for all I know.

GERRY That's bollocks, that is!

CLOUT You think so? Take me. I've always wanted a murder.

FROG 2 Like the question of colour perception, "Is what I see as green, exactly what you see as green?"

GERRY What are you going on about?

CLOUT I'm talking about a country house slaying. That would have put me on the map. I could have been "Clout of the Yard".

FROG 1 *But* the crucial point there is, we both agree that whatever it is we see when we see whatever it is *you* call "green", we both agree to call "green".

CLOUT Instead, what do I get? Stuck out here with a menopausal missus, a bunch of animal nutters and a diet of bloody spinach sandwiches.

FROG 2 Exactly. Whatever the differences in our sensory perception, we have a common linguistic accord.

FROG 1 And your point is?

GERRY Yes, what is your fucking point!?

CLOUT My point is I have nothing against animals per se. And if you were to ask me if we should be cruel or horrible to them then I'd probably say, no, I don't think we should.

FROG 2 My point is, whichever way you look at it, we're going to have to open it up and have a good old rummage round its nervous system.

GERRY Oh, that's just great!

CLOUT You say that. But if, on the other hand, you tell me that it means a lifetime of avocado and pansy sandwiches, then I'd tell you where to stick it.

CLOUT *rises to leave.*

FROG 1 Oh very well. Then let's get him ready.

The FROGS *produce leather straps and pinion* GERRY *to his chair.*

CLOUT Because the thing about animals is they just taste too good. And that's not my fault. It's just the way things are. I'll be off now, see if my men, well Toby, are in their...his... position.

GERRY No! Please! Don't leave me.

CLOUT Don't you worry, you'll be quite safe. No one can get you in here.

GERRY is securely bound to his chair.

FROG 2 leaves through the interior door, returning with a trolley laden with knives.

Don't get up. I can see myself out.

CLOUT picks up the bucket.

And I'll activate this as well, for double security.

CLOUT leaves.

GERRY Oh God!

FROG 1 Ready, Doctor?

FROG 2 Ready, Doctor.

FROG 1 Let's see these bones, shall we.

GERRY Jesus!

FROG 1 Time to meet Mummy!

*The **FROGS** pick up the knives and advance on the terrified **GERRY**.*

GERRY Okay! You win! I'll sell! I'll get out!

Blackout.

End of Act One

ACT TWO

Jago's flat

CARO *and* JAGO *are having loud, uninhibited sex.*

CARO *is barking like a dog.*

CARO I...think...it's...more...demeaning...to...dogs!

JAGO In that case maybe we should...

CARO NO!!! Don't Stop!!! Do Not Stop!!! Don't stop don't stop don't stop...

They continue lustily and very loudly whilst CLOUT *stands in the graveyard and tries to talk over them as he addresses the audience.*

CLOUT And so, to summarise... Excuse me! Don't bother about what's going on over there... Stand back! Nothing to see here! Just the sort of thing that happens all the time in a small village. It's the dark bucolic underbelly I was telling you about...

Their bestial lovemaking approaches a climax.

Hello! Everyone!!! I don't know why I bother...

CLOUT *walks off as...*

In the flat the front door bangs and CARO *and* JAGO *immediately freeze before falling down behind the sofa.*

MARC *enters. He carries a muddied spade and a sack of bones. He drops them on the floor and immediately starts undressing.*

CARO *and* JAGO*'s heads pop up from behind the sofa and then disappear behind it again.*

A scantily-clad CARO *sneaks out to the kitchen on all fours.*

JAGO, *wearing just his pants, follows her.*

But she shuts the kitchen door. He is trapped.

The now nearly-naked MARC *looks up and sees the nearly naked* JAGO.

MARC Jago? What are you doing?

JAGO Me? What am I doing? What are *you* doing?

MARC I'm getting undressed because I've just been pissed on. So what are you doing, Jago?

JAGO I'll tell you, shall I, Marc. I'll tell you what I'm doing. I'm waiting for you, *Marc*. Waiting for you to do your bit of this operation, Marc. *That's* what I'm doing. Marc.

MARC And where's your clothes?

JAGO My clothes? I'll tell you, shall I. Marc. I'll tell you. Yes. That tee shirt, *Marc*. That tee shirt you lent me, Marc, had wool in it. From a sheep, Marc. I was so, disgusted, Marc, that I...immediately... I've burnt it.

MARC And your trousers?

JAGO Everything. I couldn't take the risk.

A flushed-looking CARO *enters from the kitchen, carrying some clothes which she throws to* JAGO.

CARO Here, Jago, you can put these on.

JAGO Have they been tested for animal product?

CARO They're quite safe. Marc, what are you doing?

MARC I've been pissed on.

CARO Did you get the bones?

MARC Hello? Is anyone listening? I've been pissed on.

JAGO It was for the cause. Now, did you get the bones?

MARC Yes. She's there.

CARO *picks up the sack, weighing it in her grip.*

CARO All of her?

MARC Yes.

CARO Are you sure?

JAGO What?

CARO Well, unless the old bird's been on a diet, which seems extremely unlikely, she seems a bit light.

MARC Well that's all there was left of her.

CARO Marc? What do you mean, All there was left of her?

MARC Just that. The rest of her...the other bits...somehow... seem to be...not there. Any more. Gone.

CARO Gone? Where the hell could she have gone? Jogging?

MARC Maybe someone's dug her up.

JAGO Just what sort of maniacs are going to dig her up?

MARC Well, to be fair, Jago...

JAGO We did it for a cause.

MARC Well, maybe whoever's done it now did it for a cause.

JAGO What cause?

MARC I don't know!

CARO Calm down. It's not going to help if we start fighting amongst ourselves. Whoever's done this must have known where the new grave was. Now, if it wasn't marked what does this lead us to?

JAGO *(suddenly)* A mole!

MARC It would have to be a fucking big one.

JAGO We've been infiltrated.

CARO Except, given there's only three of us, I think we'd have noticed, don't you. But whoever it was, was dedicated. Because it takes a lot of effort to dig up a body.

MARC Don't I know it. Although...it wouldn't have taken *quite* as much effort to dig her back up again.

CARO Go on.

MARC Well...because...you know... I didn't bury her that deep.

JAGO Why not!?

MARC Because I was knackered! I'm still bloody knackered. So far I've dug her up, buried her, dug her up again and been pissed on by your father.

JAGO You weren't seen were you?

MARC No. He thought I was his mother.

JAGO That's OK then.

CARO How deep did you bury her?

MARC I don't know. A foot. Maybe?

JAGO One foot!

MARC Well I didn't see you offering to help.

CARO I might have known it! Why did I ever think that you two could be capable of doing something as simple as this without making a total pig's ear of it?

JAGO Just what have you people got against pigs?

CARO Marc, just where did you bury my grandmother one foot deep?

MARC In Pickett Woods.

CARO The woods.

MARC Yeah. No one ever goes there.

CARO No one apart from...

MARC Apart from old dears.

CARO And what do these old dears do in the woods?

MARC Nothing. Walk their... *(Realising)* ...dogs.

CARO And what to do dogs love to dig up?

MARC Fuck.

JAGO This is so bloody typical.

MARC I'm sorry, alright.

JAGO Not of you. Of *them*.

CARO Them?

JAGO Dogs. Bloody man's best bloody friends. Traitors to their
species is what dogs are. Sell out the struggle of all animal
kind for a fucking biscuit and a tummy rub, dogs will.

CARO What are you on about?

JAGO I tell you, I mean it. Dogs are the Judas Iscariots of the
animal kingdom. I've always hated them.

MARC You can't not like animals.

JAGO I can if they're dogs.

MARC So what about frogs?

JAGO I prefer them to dogs.

MARC And so if it was dogs and not frogs that were being bred
up at the Duffy farm, we'd still have dug up the old lady?

JAGO Yes, of course we would. *But* if it were dogs we were
fighting to liberate, then you can bet your life we wouldn't
have had the whole thing bollocksed up by frogs. Fucking
canine splitters.

CARO Have you two quite finished? Good. Because as Jago
has just pointed out, very correctly, this whole thing is in

severe danger of being bollocksed up. And it's up to us to make sure it isn't.

JAGO Agreed.

MARC Well said, Caro.

CARO So, we keep up the pressure on my father and uncle, telling them they won't get all the bones back until the sale of the farm has gone through.

JAGO And the frogs have been liberated.

CARO That too. So it's vital they don't realise we haven't got all of her.

JAGO Agreed.

MARC So what do we do now?

CARO "We" don't. "You two" do.

MARC We two do what?

CARO You get out there and chase every mutt you see carrying a bone in its mouth.

JAGO Both of us? Can't I mastermind it?

CARO Not this time. Boys, get out there and get those bones back for me.

MARC For us.

JAGO For the frogs. And what are you going to do?

CARO Talk to Daddy.

JAGO *and* MARC *and* CARO *leave.*

The kitchen of the Duffy farmhouse

ROGER *is sitting at the kitchen table, covered in dried mud. His hands are clasped in prayer.*

GERRY *enters.*

GERRY What are you doing?

ROGER Praying.

GERRY Not arranging another hit?

ROGER Believe it or not, I talked to our mother last night.

GERRY Really? How is she?

ROGER She...hasn't changed much. I'd had a drink and...you know... We were talking about you actually.

GERRY What are you going to get Mother to do to me?

ROGER Get you to change your mind about selling this place. Gerry, if you won't do it for your own sake, then do it for Caroline's.

GERRY Caroline?

ROGER She's scared. She's such a sensitive girl. She's worried sick about you.

GERRY About me?

He hesitates.

I've been thinking about what you said. About the six-foot frogs.

ROGER And?

GERRY And...if I do sell up. What would I do?

ROGER I've told you. Join me. It's you I'm thinking of. It's more than a lifestyle choice. It's a copper-bottomed, red hot investment opportunity.

GERRY Why doesn't anyone just talk normally anymore?

ROGER I'm telling you, this farm, financially speaking, does not wash its own face.

GERRY "Wash its own face"?

ROGER There's capital tied up here that should be working for you. For us.

GERRY I'm convinced! Mum was right about you. You are a twat. But there is something I have to tell you...

CLOUT *enters carrying a canvas sack of bones.*

CLOUT Gentlemen, I come bearing news.

GERRY *(rolling his eyes)* Oh, for God's sake!

CLOUT *(to the audience)* This is where it got *really* interesting. I hope you're all paying attention now.

GERRY *(to* CLOUT*)* Who are you talking to? Are you talking to my six-foot frogs?

ROGER *(jumping in)* You've caught them? Your ring of steel worked?

GERRY *(following* CLOUT*'s gaze towards the audience)* I'm just glad someone else can see them.

CLOUT Almost, sir.

ROGER Almost? What does that mean? Almost.

CLOUT It means partially. Bit by bit, I believe she's coming home to you. Look.

CLOUT *pulls a bone from the sack.*

GERRY What the hell's that?

CLOUT A mandible, also known as the inferior maxillary bone. And I have reason to believe it's your late mother's.

GERRY No!

CLOUT Yes!

GERRY How many bones have you got in there?

CLOUT Quite a number.

He pulls a small bone from the sack.

Now this, I can tell you, is a patella. A kneecap. But is it your mother's? Did she have particularly distinctive knees? Maybe, for example, she might have once entered or even won a knobbly knee competition.

GERRY *has pulled another bone from the sack.*

GERRY What's this one?

CLOUT That's a breast bone. I was actually going to draw a discreet veil over that one. I didn't think you'd want to be troubled by your dead mother's breasts. Or even, your mother's dead breasts. I don't know which way round is worse.

ROGER Is it relevant?

CLOUT It could be. We have to be sensitive to the feelings of the bereaved these days. Apparently they can sue.

GERRY Where did you find them all?

CLOUT They were handed in.

GERRY Who by?

CLOUT Lots of different people. It's morbid but highly public spirited of them. It was my young constable, Toby, who started putting the pieces together.

ROGER Inspector. Just who is handing in bits of mother?

CLOUT Animal lovers.

ROGER You mean the bastards who dug her up are now handing her in?

GERRY Even in death, Mother outstays her welcome.

CLOUT No, these aren't the bastards who dug her up. These are dog owners.

ROGER Mum's being dug up by dogs?

CLOUT So it would appear. Now, the human skeleton is comprised of two hundred and six bones and to date we have retrieved fifty-eight. Which means that your mother is over a quarter of the way to being fully restored to you.

GERRY Happy fucking days.

CLOUT I say fully but I must warn you, it's unlikely you'll get her all back. There are six little bones in the middle ear which could easily be swallowed by anything over a terrier.

ROGER This is appalling.

CLOUT You won't really miss them. And apart from that, it's good news.

GERRY Is it?

ROGER Yes. Yes, it is. If we get her back, or at least most of her, it means they won't have won! They won't have driven us out.

GERRY Wait a minute. I thought you wanted to get out of this place.

ROGER I did... I do... I still do but... I don't know.

GERRY Well, that's really helpful.

ROGER How can we trust them? After what they've done to Mother.

GERRY It's not like they killed her.

ROGER I know! But this is worse. They've crossed a line. They've fed Mother to the bloody dogs!

GERRY Exactly. It's like you were saying. They're maniacs and we're best off out of it. Inspector, you haven't found her head yet, have you?

CLOUT The skull? No, not yet. Why?

GERRY Just checking. Trust me, Roger, you were right. It's time to leave.

ROGER No! It's time to stay.

GERRY Roger! What about poor little Caroline?

CARO *has entered.*

CARO What about poor little Caroline? What's happened?

ROGER Caroline! My dear girl. I can't tell you. It's too horrible. Those animals have been feeding her to the dogs.

CARO Which animals?

ROGER The animals who dug her up, of course.

CARO She's been dug up by animals?

CLOUT Yes, miss, but I think he's referring to the other animals. That is to say, the animals who dug her up originally on behalf of the animals.

ROGER The bastards.

CARO Bastards?

GERRY He means the scum.

CARO I thought the police were the scum.

CLOUT No, we're the pigs.

ROGER Just where do these people think they get the right to feed my mother to the dogs.

CLOUT These days everyone has rights.

ROGER Except us.

CARO No, it's just the only rights we ever notice are other people's. And anyway, Father, it's not as if you even liked her that much.

ROGER What's that got to do with it? Since when has filial affection worked on a scale of "Love – Like – Dislike – Pet Food"?

CARO Oh stop being so emotional. And remember what you promised. We'll do anything it takes to get Granny back to us.

ROGER Well, all we have to do at the moment is whistle and say "Here Boy".

CARO So, we have to come to our senses and sell up.

GERRY She's right. Nothing can be gained from fighting these people.

CARO Except money.

ROGER Money's not everything.

CARO It could save your precious garden centre.

GERRY Save it? You told me it had a red-hot copper bottom.

ROGER It's going through a temporary cash flow situation.

CARO It's in receivership.

ROGER Temporarily.

GERRY So that's why you want me to sell this place? To save your poxy business going down the tubes!

ROGER It is *not* a poxy business! It's mine. What I've done. I made something for Caroline and for Linda and...

GERRY Now it's gone down the tubes?

ROGER Yes.

GERRY I'm sorry.

ROGER No you're not. You're smug. Because I'm right back here, where I started. With you.

GERRY That's why I'm sorry.

ROGER Well, alright then, I'm staying. With you.

GERRY We'll sell.

ROGER No. We'll fight. And anyway, who in their right mind would buy this place?

CARO For your information, there's an interested party ready to make us a very handsome offer.

ROGER Who?

CARO *(vaguely)* I don't know. Some people. They take care of animals.

CLOUT Like a sanctuary?

CARO That sort of thing. So, Daddy. You have a choice. Give in to these maniacs, sell this place and make me happy.

Pause.

ROGER Or? You said I had a choice.

CARO Figure of speech. Keeping thinking Daddy. Keep thinking and don't stop.

CLOUT What?

CARO Don't stop!!!

She leaves.

CLOUT *clicks his fingers and* **ROGER** *and* **GERRY** *freeze.*
CLOUT *addresses the audience.*

CLOUT "Don't stop". I'd heard that before... How did it go? Don't stop... Don't stop... Harder! Harder... Don't stop... (**CLOUT** *starts barking like an orgasmic dog)* Yes, that was it. I thought it was time to pay a little visit to Miss Duffy.

He clicks his fingers. **ROGER** *and* **GERRY** *unfreeze and the scene continues.*

You two obviously have a lot to talk about and so I won't intrude any longer.

He goes to leave but remembers something.

But whilst, I'm here, I'll take that cutting.

Before **GERRY** *or* **ROGER** *can say anything,* **CLOUT** *has snipped a cutting from the cannabis plant.*

Mrs Clout is getting quite impatient to get it planted. If she has any luck with it, you'll be the first to know.

CLOUT *leaves.*

GERRY I bet we will. Come on, brother. We're out of here.

ROGER No.

GERRY No? No?! What do you mean "no"?

ROGER I refuse to be driven out of my home.

GERRY Suddenly you live here?

ROGER Anyway, I thought you were the one who wanted to stay.

GERRY And you were the one who wanted to go. Well, you were right, I was wrong. We're going, we're selling, we're out of here.

ROGER No!

GERRY But...but...he's got the cutting. Clout has the stuff! As soon as his wife tries to make a tomato salad out of that... he comes home, she's off her tits, the whole game's up!

ROGER I don't care.

GERRY You will. You own half of this place. You are half responsible for all that gear in there.

ROGER I don't care. How did we get here? To this? This is *my* country!

GERRY It's a few other people's as well.

ROGER Giving in to the bully boys and extremists. Is this what Mother would have wanted?

GERRY Of course it is! Mother was the most extreme bully of them all. And anyway, what about Caroline? I thought you'd promised her.

ROGER Caroline's like her mother.

GERRY Promiscuous?

ROGER Headstrong. Proud. But she'll understand. One day, she'll see I'm doing it for her. I tell you, brother, life has been slowly but surely pushing us into a corner. And when you're in a corner and your back's to the wall, that's when you turn and fight.

GERRY *(sotto)* Twat.

Jago's flat

MARC *and* JAGO *enter carrying a sack of bones. They are exhausted and flop down onto the sofa.*

CARO *storms in.*

CARO What are you two doing?

JAGO We're exhausted.

MARC I was severely menaced by a cocker spaniel.

JAGO Although he was perfectly within his rights to defend his territory from unwarranted human incursion. Agreed?

MARC Agreed. Although he was a nasty fucker.

JAGO Agreed. So stick the kettle on, Caro.

CARO Since when do you order me around?

MARC Well, he is the leader.

CARO Leader!?

JAGO Tell you what, I'll go and put it on.

CARO It's thanks to his "leadership" and your pathetic, amateur bumbling that this whole deal is now in jeopardy.

JAGO They're still going to liberate the frogs, aren't they? They can't go back on the agreement.

CARO What agreement? They've already got half of her back! I mean, how difficult is it to kidnap an old woman who's been dead for five years and not let her escape and start roaming the countryside?

MARC What are we going to do?

There is a knock at the door.

JAGO Who the hell's that?

MARC I don't know.

CARO It's probably just...the milkman.

JAGO We don't drink milk.

The knocking comes again.

CLOUT *(from outside)* Open up! It's the police!

JAGO Shit!

CARO Hide.

JAGO Good thinking.

JAGO *and* MARC *dive behind the sofa.*

CARO Not you! The bones!

JAGO Yes! Right.

The knocking comes again.

Where?

CARO Anywhere. I'll try and stall him.

CARO *goes to the hallway and calls out as* JAGO *and* MARC *empty the sack of bones into the sofa.*

Hello? Who is it?

CLOUT *(from outside)* The police. Can you open the door?

CARO I'm just in the shower. Can you come back later?

CLOUT *(from outside)* I'll wait.

CARO *exits, undressing as she goes.* MARK *and* JAGO *continue stuffing bones under the cushions of the sofa.*

(from outside) Are you out yet?

CARO *(offstage)* Nearly.

Now wrapped in a towel, CARO *pokes her head round the door.*

Have you two finished?

JAGO *gives her the thumbs up and she goes to let* CLOUT *in.*

CLOUT Sorry to disturb you, miss.

CARO Well, it's not very convenient, Inspector Clout. I was in the shower.

CLOUT Really? You don't appear to be very moist.

CARO I beg your pardon!

CLOUT Who's this then?

CARO These are my friends...flatmates. These are my flatmates.

MARC Hello.

CLOUT You all live here together, do you?

CARO I don't see that's any of your business.

CLOUT You're right, it's not. However, I wasn't making an enquiry of your domestic morals, so much as querying why one of these gentlemen couldn't have opened the door.

CARO Good question.

CLOUT Well?

JAGO We can't. We're...

MARC ...agoraphobic.

CLOUT Good answer.

MARC Thank you.

CARO What can we do for you, Inspector? I'm assuming there must be a reason for your hammering so threateningly on our front door.

CLOUT Sorry about that. Force of habit. Or rather, habit of the force. *(Beat)* Please yourselves.

CARO That could be viewed as police intimidation.

CLOUT Ah no, no, no. We're all community oriented, these days. Empathising with the criminal's point of view, dropping round for friendly little chats, being invited in for a cup of tea... *(To* CARO*)* ...don't mind if I do, miss. Milk and two sugars.

CARO *rolls her eyes and exits.*

Much obliged. It's apparently good for us to get to know those whom it is our pleasure and privilege to protect and serve. To sit down, make ourselves comfortable and...

CLOUT *sits on the sofa. There is a cracking of bones. He reaches behind and produces a tibia from under his cushion.*

JAGO So that's where it got to. I've been looking for that.

CLOUT Yours is it?

JAGO Yes.

CLOUT *looks at* JAGO*'s two legs.*

That is, yes in the sense of I found it. And I believe that possession is nine tenths of the law. Isn't that right, Inspector?

CLOUT I'd say that depends on what it is that's possessed, wouldn't you? Where did you come by it? Do you own a dog?

JAGO Do you mean, does a dog share our living space and accept our food and shelter, whilst retaining its rights, identity and sovereignty as a free animal?

CLOUT No, I mean, do you own a dog?

JAGO A human being cannot "own" a dog.

CLOUT No, that's cats you're thinking of. But I take it you don't own a dog.

JAGO No, I do not.

CLOUT Then perhaps you can tell me just where you got that...

CLOUT *pulls out the rest of the bones from the sofa.*

...and this...and these.

He piles them all up on the table.

MARC   The things you find down the back of the sofa, eh! We're really going to have to have a word with the cleaner.

CLOUT   Well?

MARC   The dogs found them.

CLOUT   What dogs? He said you don't own a dog.

JAGO   We don't. But...we walk dogs.

MARC   That's right. We run a dog-walking service.

CLOUT   Even though you're agoraphobic?

JAGO   We only take them for very short walks.

CLOUT   I see.

MARC   Do you?

CLOUT   Not really. And what were you planning on doing with these pieces of evidence?

JAGO   Evidence of what? The fact that dogs like bones? I thought even the British police force had worked that one out by now.

MARC   We were going to hand them in, of course.

CLOUT   That's very public spirited of you. I'll take them with me when I go. Lucky I dropped by, wasn't it?

MARC   *(unhappily)* Yes. Wasn't it.

CARO, *now dressed, enters with a mug of tea.*

CARO   Sorry, we never use milk.

CLOUT   Never? Why not? What's wrong with good, natural, healthy cow's milk?

CARO Nothing.

CLOUT Oh well, not to worry. I'll have it black.

CLOUT takes a foil packet of sandwiches from his pocket.

But I need a bit of a wet whilst I eat my lunch. I've got a nervous digestive system. Have to eat punctually otherwise there's hell to pay.

JAGO What have you got there?

CLOUT Just my sandwiches.

JAGO What's in them?

CLOUT Nice juicy bit of ham. Made them myself.

JAGO Disgusting.

CLOUT Lovely. Fresh off the bone. All pink and succulent. With a bit of fat still clinging to it. Would you like one?

JAGO I don't eat animals.

CLOUT You mean meat? Really? Very interesting. And why's that then?

JAGO Quite apart from the health considerations, there is no moral justification for human beings feasting on the flesh of other species.

CLOUT Is that right?

JAGO Yes. That's right.

CLOUT Well, I'm just an officer of the law and so morality has never really been my strong suit. I've always seen it as a bit of a fad.

CARO What? Morality?

CLOUT And vegetarianism. I mean, liking animals is one thing. I like animals. Particularly this one, which is very tasty. Are you sure you won't?

JAGO Do you have a point, Inspector?

CLOUT I suppose my point is, no one has the right to force others to agree with them. Wouldn't you agree? And I must warn you, failure to agree with that could result in criminal prosecution.

MARC That's not fair.

CLOUT Fair? No, you've lost me again. I'm not sure this life is meant to be fair, sir. It's a dog eat dog world.

CARO Or in this case, pig eat pig.

CLOUT That's very good, that. But all jocular banter aside for a moment, we're living in a time of dangerous extremism. Fanaticism stalks the land with what some might describe as *grave* consequences. And I have to admit, the situation here gives me cause for disquiet.

CARO What situation is that, exactly?

CLOUT The idea of three strict vegetarians sharing a flat together.

JAGO That's become a crime now, has it?

CLOUT It's almost a terrorist cell, in my book.

JAGO Is everyone you don't agree with "a terrorist cell"? Are we suddenly "Vegan Fundamentalists"?

CARO Excuse me, Inspector?

She takes a sandwich and calmly bites into it.

JAGO Are we the new victims of the so-called war against... what are you doing Caro?

CARO Don't mind me. Carry on. It's very interesting. And delicious, Inspector.

MARC Actually, don't mind if I do.

MARC *takes a sandwich and wolfs it down hungrily.*

CLOUT It seems as though I'd got it wrong about you lot.

JAGO You're not the only one.

CLOUT Well, I think I'll bid you all farewell whilst I still have some lunch left.

CARO Thank you for popping round, Inspector. You may have got me wrong but you should never underestimate me.

CLOUT I'll try not to, miss. Good day to you all.

CLOUT *leaves with the bones.*

JAGO What the hell do you think you're doing? How can you two bring yourself to eat that innocent, defenceless creature?

CARO I did it for the cause. You saw how suspicious he was. We had to throw him off the scent and as far as I was concerned, it was us or the pig.

JAGO Caro, you're right. *(To* MARC*)* So what was your excuse? Caro had selflessly sacrificed her principles for the greater good. You didn't have to as well.

MARC I was hungry.

JAGO What!?

MARC I've been doing all the digging.

JAGO That's no justification for gorging on the dead flesh of the innocent.

MARC It was only a bloody sandwich.

JAGO That's what the Nazis said at Nuremberg.

CARO Jago! Can we please get back to the business of getting my stupid bloody father to agree to the sale of the sodding farm. We are running out of time. Think of the frogs! We need a plan B.

JAGO Have we got a plan B?

CARO We have now.

There is a moment's pause then all three of them start trashing the flat.

Jago's flat

A blue light is flashing from outside.

CLOUT *is talking into a dictaphone as he looks around.*

CLOUT Miss Duffy was abducted sometime between when her flatmates left to take a dog for a walk at 4.15 and when they returned at 4.17. I hope those two don't charge too much. There are no signs of forced entry. However, there are obvious signs of a struggle. Or they really do need a serious talk with their cleaner.

CLOUT *moves the cushions on the sofa as he says this and sees something inside it.*

Talking of which... Hello, what do we have here? Is it? ...Yes! It is!

He brings out a skull from inside the sofa.

Oh, sorry Toby, you're probably wondering what's going on. Well, I have just found a skull, a human skull, down the back of the sofa. I obviously missed it on my last visit here.

Actually, let's not make too much of a thing about that, shall we. In fact, forget I said it. Good.

CLOUT *sits on the sofa, contemplating the skull.*

The lights dim on him and he stays there throughout the next scene.

The Duffy farmhouse

In the darkness Roger is on the phone.

ROGER *(into the phone)* How is she? Is she alright? Tell me she's alright. If you do anything to her...

JAGO *is heard on stage but unseen.*

JAGO Whatever happens to your precious daughter, I can promise you she won't be poisoned, raped or brutalised. All the things you and your sort do to innocent frogs.

ROGER *(to himself)* "Raped"?

JAGO But anything that does happen to her will be your doing. Not us, you.

ROGER What are you on about?

JAGO You have the power to stop this. You blame us but we're only doing what you're making us do. You bear the responsibility. Understand?

ROGER Yes. I understand.

JAGO Good.

ROGER And I want you to understand what it is that you're making me do. Your responsibility. I will close down our farm.

JAGO Good.

ROGER I will end our business.

JAGO Good.

ROGER But you're not getting our frogs. How much do you know about frogs?

JAGO I know they have the unalienable right to live without fear, stress or torture.

ROGER As I thought, nothing. So, let me tell you a couple of things about frogs. For example, did you know that whilst, unlike you, frogs don't have very highly developed morals about eating other living things, they actually don't need to drink. This is because they absorb water through their skins. And also they don't sweat. Isn't that interesting.

JAGO Is there a point to any of this?

ROGER A question I ask myself constantly. But yes, in this case there actually is.

JAGO Go on.

ROGER The point is, I'm about to tell you what it is that you are making me do. What it is that you are going to have on your conscience.

JAGO Go on.

ROGER I'm going to boil them. All of them. Alive.

JAGO You can't do that! Frogs have got rights.

The lights slowly start to cross-fade from ROGER *to* JAGO, *standing in the flat, on the phone, smoking a joint and getting more paranoid by the second.*

ROGER We've all got rights. Until we lose them. And the truth is it's terrifyingly easy. I want you to picture a big, gunmetal grey pan of water sitting on a stove. Calm, cool and placid. Now, you turn up the heat under it and before you know it, you've got a boiling, spitting, angry sea. You throw a frog into that and they are going to leap straight out again, away from the pain and the danger.

Not a pretty image, is it? A scalded frog, trying to hop its way to freedom and a life free of stress, fear and torture.

JAGO You're a maniac. You can't do that.

ROGER Calm down. I know I can't. *That* is the point. If one is going to boil one frog, let alone five thousand, that's not the way one goes about it. So let me tell you how to boil a frog. Go back to the gunmetal grey pan, waiting on the stove. Can you see it? The cool, inviting water. Well, what you do is slip your frog into that. He won't mind. You see, he's a frog and, if you didn't know, he can live as well in the water as he can on the land. And so he's quite happy in there. And then you turn on the heat.

Just low at first. Raise the temperature by slow degrees. Cool to tepid to lukewarm to warmish and then to warm. But you keep on going. Warm turns to hot. When is the danger sensed? At what point does panic start? Because it's such a slow, gradual change from bearable to uncomfortable to unbearable, poor old Mr Frog never twigs. He should have done something about it before. He should have fought back. Defended his rights. But now it's too late. They've gone. And the pain he feels now has been a part of him for so long, its creeping inevitability has now encased him and he is boiled alive.

So now do you see the point?

JAGO *throws the phone down.*

JAGO Aarrrgh!

CARO What's happened?

JAGO Your father's mad.

CARO I meant more recently.

JAGO He's going on the rampage. We have to stop him.

MARC I don't have to do any more digging, do I?

JAGO *takes a coil of rope from a rucksack, which he throws to* MARC.

JAGO Tie her up.

MARC *(shocked)* Jago!

JAGO And don't use my name when we're on an operation.

CARO But your name's Graham.

JAGO Shut it, Posh Girl! *(To* MARC*)* On an operation it's Jago. And don't forget it. Or use it. Now, tie her up. If he's going to play psycho, then we'll play psycho.

The kitchen of the Duffy farmhouse

ROGER *is cleaning a doubled-barrelled shotgun. On the table in front of him is a lethal array of knives, a scythe, a bill hook, a poker.*

GERRY *enters holding a suit case and a cane toad.*

GERRY Roger, I don't wish to alarm you but it's getting bloody hot back there.

ROGER Everyone has their boiling point.

GERRY Well, I think the frogs are about to reach theirs.

ROGER Good.

GERRY *surveys the weaponry on the table.*

GERRY Expecting company, are we? And I thought my entertaining skills were rusty. Look, I don't know whether you know this or not, but these days the law no longer sides with the homicidal farmer.

ROGER When they break in here they'll get what's coming to them.

GERRY And so will you. I know it's a hideous attack on tradition but you can no longer slaughter foxes, badgers, or animal rights activists. Roger, you can't do this.

ROGER Whether you like it or not, we have to do this. We have to fight for our rights.

GERRY You really do believe that shit, don't you? "Fight for our rights". You'll be telling me next that an Englishman's home is his castle, all's fair in love and war and everyone's innocent until proven guilty.

ROGER Not everyone.

GERRY No, I forgot. Of course not everyone. God forbid *everyone* should join in this mad stampede for civil liberties. I mean, if everyone had freedom there might not be enough to go around. And then what would happen to *you* and *your* precious rights?

ROGER I haven't got any bloody rights!!!

GERRY No one's got any bloody rights!!!

ROGER That's rich coming from you. You always said...

GERRY No. It's all come clear at last. *This* is the benefit of a lifetime spent sitting on your arse. Finally you sort stuff out.

ROGER And you've sorted it out, have you?

GERRY Yes.

ROGER Okay. This should be good.

GERRY Human rights are like male nipples.

ROGER What?!

GERRY Bear with me. It's good this. You and I, we have nipples, right?

ROGER Right.

GERRY All men are born with nipples. We'd hate to lose them and we fight to keep them. *But* we have no idea how we got them or what we can do with them. And it's only when we try to use them that we realise just what a pointless adornment they really are.

Pause.

ROGER And?

GERRY And...it's the same with rights. Just because we've got them, it doesn't mean we can do anything with them.

Pause. ROGER *looks at him.*

ROGER And that's it is it? A lifetime on your arse and the best you can come up with is nipples?

GERRY Have you got anything better?

ROGER *considers. He hasn't.*

ROGER So...what do we do?

GERRY We do...

> GERRY *takes a suck of the cane toad.*

GERRY ...whatever the fuck we like, brother.

ROGER Right.

> *The brothers high-five as outside the door bangs open.*

ROGER Let's do it.

> ROGER *takes the tablecloth from the table and he and* GERRY *stand either side of the door.* CLOUT *enters and they throw the cloth over his head and wrestle him to the floor.*

CLOUT Help! Police!!!

ROGER Too late to call for them now.

CLOUT I'm not calling for them. I *am* them.

> CLOUT *struggles from under the cloth.*

ROGER Inspector Clout. What a treat to see you.

CLOUT You say that now, sir, but I'm afraid I'm here on serious matters.

ROGER Serious? You? Surely not.

CLOUT Oh yes. I'm afraid I come bearing...

> CLOUT *holds out the skull towards* GERRY.

...this!

GERRY Fuck me! It's Hamlet.

CLOUT Not quite. But apparently I am a player in a tragedy.

ROGER What have you got there? It's not...is it?

CLOUT Yes it is. And I have every reason to believe that it is your late mother's.

ROGER So she's very nearly all home with us.

GERRY *takes the skull and stares at it.*

CLOUT That's what I had hoped. But then this turned up. And was examined by my constable, Toby.

GERRY Or not Toby.

CLOUT No. Toby.

He takes the skull back from GERRY.

And he's uncovered something rather puzzling, which sheds a disturbing light on the way your late mother met her end.

ROGER I know how my mother met her end, Inspector.

CLOUT You do?

ROGER Yes, I do. It was me, Inspector. I had her struck down. And it has haunted me ever since.

CLOUT A confession!

GERRY Inspector, if a man can't murder his own mother then who can he murder?

CLOUT I'll have to refer your enquiry to more subtle legal minds than my own. However, in the meantime, Roger Duffy, I'm arresting you for murder. Yes! I can't tell you how long I've waited to hear myself say those words.

ROGER But, Inspector Clout, it was an act of God.

CLOUT We'll charge him as an accessory if you like but I don't think a jury will buy it. Because if it was the hand of God...

CLOUT *removes the top of the skull.*

...it was rather heavy handed of him. As you can see, the top of the skull has been battered in with some blunt instrument, such as a shovel, a brick or maybe a poker.

GERRY *is standing there holding a poker. He immediately hides it behind his back.*

ROGER So what happens now? Am I going to go to prison?

CLOUT Well...yes...in the normal run of things, I expect that's what would happen.

ROGER And this isn't the normal of run of things?

CLOUT Well, it was a long time ago. Maybe, it could be worth everyone's while not to go digging up old bones. Obviously, though, when I say "worth everyone's while" I mean it would have to be worth someone's slightly more than others.

GERRY Meaning?

CLOUT Meaning I've given a lifetime of service to the general public.

GERRY But you've never caught many criminals.

CLOUT It's not my fault! I've put the hours in. And for what? Everything I've done for the last five years of my life has been to do with you and this place and frogs and extremists and keeping the peace and the village in turmoil and...and now you think you can just cash in, do you? Take the money and run and leave me here with nothing to show for it? Do you? Is that what you think? Well, I know where the bodies are buried. *(Beat)* Even if they're not buried there anymore.

ROGER Are you trying to blackmail us, Clout?

CLOUT Blackmail is an ugly word for a delicate procedure.

GERRY So is "cunnilingus" but once it's said we all know what we're talking about.

CLOUT Seeing as how having principles hasn't got me anywhere, I figure corruption is an area of law enforcement that would be a shame not to experience before I retire. And if you two can sell out then so can I.

ROGER How much do you want?

CLOUT I've always liked to think I'm not a greedy man but now I've just discovered the shocking truth that I am. All of it.

GERRY But what if we don't sell? After all, Mother's returned. Albeit to haunt us.

CLOUT Oh, I think you will. Because apart from the small matter of murder, don't forget they've also got his daughter. And I'm sure you won't want her returned to you in bits.

ROGER He's right. We are going to sell.

GERRY And give him all the money? I've held out for three years of living hell, to finally sell up and then give the money to fucking Colombo here? What next!

JAGO and MARC enter. They wear the frog masks from the first scene. They are both holding wooden clubs and have CARO between them. She is bound and with the sack over her head.

Oh, brilliant! These are the six-foot frogs I was telling you about. Now, I know you can't see them, but don't worry. I've discovered whatever they do you'll wake up tomorrow just fine.

JAGO viciously bludgeons ROGER to the floor with his club.

ROGER Ahhh!

GERRY Now, that's not really happening.

JAGO clubs GERRY.

Ow fuck!!! No, that really did hurt!

ROGER Caroline.

CARO Daddy?

JAGO Stand back, you.

JAGO draws a large knife and holds it to CARO's throat.

Take another move and I'll...

GERRY You'll what?

JAGO She'll get it.

CARO Ow! Not so hard. Daddy! Do what they say. Please. They mean it.

ROGER They're just full of talk.

JAGO The time for talking is over. You had your chance and now we're not talking to you anymore.

MARC And that's our last word.

ROGER So what do you want now?

MARC We're...not telling you.

JAGO Yes we are.

MARC Are we?

JAGO Yes. Free the frogs.

ROGER Release my daughter.

JAGO Not 'till the frogs are free.

GERRY Roger, you can see the six-foot frogs? Have you been sucking my toads?

JAGO Do it or I'll cut her. I mean it! I'll do it!

MARC Jago...

CARO (*scared*) Daddy!

MARC Jago, you're scaring her.

JAGO Keep out of it.

MARC Leave her alone.

JAGO Don't betray the cause.

MARC Fuck the cause. I love her.

JAGO That's the difference between us, Marc. I love the cause and it's her I fuck.

CLOUT Can someone tell me what's going on?

MARC Jago... Caro? How could you?

ROGER Caro?

JAGO When you were digging up bones, I was burying mine.

CARO It was never anything personal.

MARC You fucking bastard!

MARC *leaps on* **JAGO** *and they start fighting.*

GERRY You know this doesn't usually happen.

CLOUT Don't get involved. In my professional experience, in a contest between an unarmed frog and one with a knife, always bet on the knife.

CARO Oh, for God's sake!

She tears the sack from her head.

ROGER Caroline, what the hell is happening here?

CARO Just what does it take for you to do the smart thing? Just for once in your life.

JAGO That's right. Free the frogs!

CARO Fuck the frogs! Sell the farm.

JAGO Excuse me! Point of order! "Fuck the frogs"? What kind of talk is that?

CARO Oh, not now.

JAGO Am I to understand that you are somehow using the vernacular for human procreation to attempt to denigrate the frog? Because, personally speaking, I find frogs attractive. I love animals.

CARO No, Graham, hating people is not the same as loving animals.

JAGO It's bloody close!

CARO Father, boil the slimy, sexless lumps of hopping snot. And then, when you're done, sign the papers and take the cash!

MARC Caro, I'm starting to have serious doubts about your commitment to the cause.

ROGER The cause? What bloody cause? Caroline?

JAGO I'll go further. I move that we start immediate emergency procedures to expel Caro from the movement.

MARC I'm reluctantly forced to agree.

JAGO So you have to say "seconded".

MARC Do I?

JAGO Yes.

MARC Okay then, seconded. Now then, you fucker!

MARC charges at JAGO – they both smash through the interior door – the brilliant white light shines out where they have gone. GERRY is mesmerised by the light.

ROGER Caroline, for God's sake. Tell me you're not involved with these...animals. You're not one of the maniacs?

CARO How else was I going to get you to sell this place?

ROGER But digging up your own grandmother!

CARO You must admit, it was nearly very effective. Only I forgot just *how* much you hated the old cow.

JAGO *(offstage)* There's nothing hateful about cows!

CARO And just *how* guilty it made you feel. And anyway, none of this would have happened if you two had just agreed to sell up and give me my share of the money.

ROGER So it's our fault?

CARO Of course it is.

ROGER Caroline, you can't go around blaming everyone else for this.

CARO It's not my fault I blame everyone else. It's yours.

ROGER You're no daughter of mine!

CARO Fine! Whatever. Look, Father, Did you read that offer from the Happy Chick Corporation? We'd be mad not to take it!

CLOUT The what?

CARO The Happy Chick Corporation. Suppliers to every major supermarket chain and fast food outlet in Western Europe.

ROGER They supply chickens?

CARO And eggs.

CLOUT Which did they do first?

ROGER But you told me that they take care of animals.

CARO They do. Bloody effectively. On a site this size they reckon they could turn out between forty and sixty thousand birds a day.

CLOUT That's a lot of drumsticks.

ROGER So you're saying that they're going to turn this place into a chicken farm?

CARO Farm, factory. It's difficult to say. But they're looking for a quick deal and are prepared to pay over the odds to anyone desperate to sell. And Daddy, they are giving us four million excellent reasons to sell this dump.

CLOUT Four million quid! Christ! Why have I never tried corruption before?

ROGER All this is just about money?

CARO What else is there? Your business fails, Mum leaves you. It's all about money.

ROGER So what happens to society? If everyone behaves like this? Like animals.

CARO We *are* all animals. The only difference is we pretend to be something better. But we're not. We're cruel, greedy, stupid and selfish. We have no rights, no obligations, no duty to anyone or anything. Welcome to the farm, Daddy! It's sell or be sold.

ROGER Okay! You win! You always win. We are going to sell.

CARO Halleh-bloody-lujah!

ROGER *But* my darling, stupid, selfish, greedy girl, thanks to you...there isn't any money.

CARO What?

ROGER You dug up the bones.

CLOUT What your father's saying is that uncovering is easy but it's always the cover-up that costs.

ROGER If we don't pay him, then I'm going to prison.

CARO What for?

CLOUT Murder.

CARO You killed Granny!?

ROGER Only with divine intervention. I didn't think anything was actually going to happen.

GERRY *(suddenly)* Natural causes!

CLOUT Is he still here?

CARO Only just.

GERRY That's what did for the old girl. Natural causes.

GERRY *wields the poker like a scimitar.*

Smack! Crack! Wallop!

ROGER Natural causes?

GERRY You bet. I tell you, you crack a seventy-six-year-old over the nut with a poker, it's completely natural that she dies.

CLOUT Are you saying that you killed her?

ROGER No! No, I killed her.

GERRY Smack! Crack! Wallop! You believed you did!

CLOUT But I've already got a confession! I don't need another one.

GERRY But you didn't have the skull. Smack! Crack! Wallop!

ROGER But why? Why did *you* kill her?

GERRY She was about to tell you about us.

ROGER Us?

GERRY We never wanted you to know. Me and Linda.

ROGER You and... Linda?! My wife, Linda?

CARO My mother, Linda?

CLOUT My girlfriend, Linda!

ROGER That bloody woman. Linda. She burnt my heart to a fucking cinder!

GERRY *That's* the rhyme I've been looking for! Look, we did try to resist. Just not very hard. You said she's no daughter of yours.

CARO You'd better not be saying I'm a daughter of yours.

ROGER You bastard!

ROGER *launches himself at* GERRY *and they fight.*

GERRY I don't know if I'm her dad. Not for sure. Linda managed to narrow it down a bit.

ROGER Narrow it down!?

GERRY A bit, yes. There was a list.

ROGER Was I on it?

GERRY Of course. Just not very near the top. I always liked to think it was me. Sorry to break it to you like this only there's never really been a good time to tell you before.

ROGER And now's a good time?

GERRY It's the best there's been yet.

ROGER What did she see in you? You've never done anything with your life!

GERRY Excuse me! I did at least kill our mother.

They fight until they see MARC *and* JAGO *wander in through the light of the interior door. They have taken their frog masks off and are smoking huge joints.*

Oh my God! Six-foot-people!

MARC Caro. How could you betray us all like this?

CARO Coming from this family, what do you expect? Sorry, Marc, but the only way I could get you to do what I wanted was to not sleep with you.

MARC But what about him. He's mental enough to have done anything without you fucking him. Why did you have to sleep with Jago?

CARO To annoy my father, of course! That's what girls like me always do.

ROGER Well, it's bloody well worked!

MARC You bitch!

MARC *launches himself at* CARO.

ROGER She may be a bitch but she's my daughter. I think.

ROGER *leaps in to save* CARO *from* MARC.

JAGO It's...unbelievable! It's...amazing...through there...there's so *much of* it! It's like wall to wall "Toad". It's...brilliant!

GERRY You're a customer?

CARO But Marc, you've won! They're selling this place and I've lost. I'm not getting the money.

JAGO No! No, we've got to keep this place going. There's "Toad". Loads of it.

MARC But I'm not getting you!

GERRY I'm glad you like it.

ROGER Are you sure you want her?

JAGO I love it. It's like...the best.

MARC I loved you!!!

> **JAGO** *and* **GERRY** *embrace as* **ROGER, CARO** *and* **MARC** *fight.*

JAGO How do you do it? What's the secret?

GERRY Cane toad venom.

JAGO No!!! It's an animal product!

> *He launches himself at* **GERRY.**

You bastard!

GERRY Can someone tell me. Is this bit real? Is this actually happening?

> *They all fight.*

> *Throughout the scene the sound of the boiling frogs has been growing. Suddenly there is an almighty cacophony of squelching bangs – screams from* **ROGER, GERRY, CARO, MARC** *and* **JAGO** *– and the crash of the farmhouse collapsing.*

> **CLOUT** *is alone on stage holding the shotgun.*

CLOUT They had our ballistic boys test-firing frogs for weeks after the tragedy. You'd be shocked at the damage a super-heated, fully inflated bull frog can inflict. It can punch a hole in a man the size of a small melon.

Apart from myself, the only person to be pulled alive from the wreckage of the farmhouse was the terrorist...

> *He takes out a library card and reads it.*

...Graham "Jago" Elliston. However, he refused to allow paramedics to dress his wounds, believing that Elastoplasts had been developed using animal research. He was wrong and bled to death in the ambulance.

The Happy Chick Corporation was happier than usual, as all its demolition costs had been taken care of by exploding frogs. Its Happy Hatchery is now home to eighty thousand happy little chickens. No natural light and their beaks sheared off to stop them fighting and damaging investment.

Under this speech the terrible sound of eighty thousand chickens in a battery shed starts to slowly build.

It sounds cruel. It probably is cruel. But it's highly temporary. Thirty-six days and they're put on the killing line and stunned, killed, plucked, gutted, frozen and on the truck under thirty-seven minutes.

It's quite an operation. And I should know because now I've really found my metier. Head of security of the Happiest Hatchery in Western Europe. It's so much more satisfying than police work.

Because it's like the lady said...

He cocks the shotgun. The noise echoes round the auditorium.

...welcome to the farm.

With a smile he turns and is gone.

The ghastly sound of the chickens rises until...

Blackout.

...And silence.

PROPERTY LIST

ACT ONE

Pick axe
Muddied spades x 2
Toy frog masks for Marc and Jago
Femur (human thigh bone)
Library card
Cannabis plants – several
Old guitar for Gerry
Poker
Tea towel
Police evidence bag
Tin bucket
Pair of very dark glasses for Gerry
Bath towel for Jago
Notebook and pen for Jago
Scales for weighing cannabis
Knife for cutting cannabis
Cannabis resin
Small tank for cane toad
Cane toad
Clipboard and pen for frog 2
Long needle for frog 2
Cordless telephone for Gerry's kitchen
Old style video camera
Pad of paper and pen for Jago
House brick
Mobile phone for Clout
Long pole with hook on the end
Scissors for Clout
Foil packet of sandwiches for Clout
Leather restraints
Trolley laden with knives

ACT TWO

Muddied spade
Sack of bones for Marc and Jago
Clothes for Jago
Canvas sack of bones for Clout
Mandible (lower jaw bone)
Patella (kneecap)
Sternum (breast bone)
Cannabis plant
Scissors for Clout
Large bath towel for Caro
Tibia (shin bone)
Assorted human bones
Mug of tea
Foil packet of sandwiches for Clout
Dictaphone for Clout
Skull (with detachable top)
Cordless phone for Gerry's kitchen
Mobile phone for Jago
Rucksack
Coil of rope
Double-barrelled shotgun
Knives
Scythe
Bill hook
Poker
Suitcase for Gerry
Cane toad
Table cloth
Toy frog masks for Marc and Jago
Wooden clubs x 2
Sack
Large knife for Jago
Large cannabis joints for Marc and Jago
Library card for Clout

THIS
IS
NOT
THE
END

Lightning Source UK Ltd.
Milton Keynes UK
UKOW05f1949240117
292791UK00005B/9/P